Abo

The author as Gay Daventry in Ivor Novello's 'Gay's The Word'.

Stage-struck, from the age of four, I trained as a dancer, but after an ankle injury in my mid-teens, I devoted my energies to things of a more academic nature. At the age of eighteen, instead of going off to ballet school, I went to university and read physics and maths. A neighbour of my mother's said, "No one should have been surprised because Jean was always very physical."

For forty-plus years, my working life was in the world of education: teacher, headteacher, Trade Union General Secretary, then eight years as a borough councillor, including one year as the Mayor, but my spare time was reserved for extracurricular speaking engagements and my theatrical activities. I've performed in, choreographed and/or directed well over two hundred operas, plays, musicals, concerts and pageants and recently compered my first Zoom concert.

LOOK BACK WITH LAUGHTER

Within the constraints of an octogenarian's memory, all my anecdotes are true.

JEAN GEMMELL

LOOK BACK WITH LAUGHTER

Vanguard Press

A CIP catalogue record for this title is
available from the British Library.

ISBN 978 1 80016 338 6

*Vanguard Press is an imprint of
Pegasus Elliot Mackenzie Publishers Ltd.*
www.pegasuspublishers.com

First Published in 2022

**Vanguard Press
Sheraton House Castle Park
Cambridge England**

Printed & Bound in Great Britain

Dedication

To all the friends, family, acquaintances and complete
strangers who feature in my tales, as well as everyone
who has patiently listened to them over the years,
especially those who encouragingly laughed.

Acknowledgements

For enabling my storytelling to reach a wider
audience:

Alice, who assisted my first steps online,

Ann, whose interest and appreciation encouraged
me to venture into print,

and Peter who made it all work for me.

Contents

The Hazards of the Boards

1. Overture and Beginners

Hello, everyone. I thought I might try to entertain you by telling you a story. For some years now I've been entertaining groups such as Women's Institutes by acting as a raconteur and sharing with them some of the amusing aspects of the various things that I have done in my life. In recent weeks, of course, that activity has been curtailed, so I thought it might be fun for me, and I hope for you the listener and reader if I tried doing it 'online', as they say.

Some of you may be old enough to remember what Anderson shelters were. They were half-cylinders, usually made of corrugated iron and buried under the ground — just under the topsoil you understand — and they were put there as air-raid shelters. I was born in Chatham, in Kent. Chatham, a very famous dockyard town, was very heavily bombed during the Second World War, and my grandparents had such a shelter in their back garden. One night, the air-raid siren went off and everybody went down into the shelter. My grandfather was a sprightly sort of chap and he got there first; my mother handed to him what he took to be an ill-assorted bundle of bedding, he grabbed it rather unceremoniously and I fell out! I, being just a very small baby at the time, my mother, as you might imagine, panicked. But my mother's friend was part of the party in the shelter, and she assured my mother that since baby's heads weren't properly formed anyway, landing on the hard-packed earth floor wasn't likely to have done any lasting damage. If I tell you that my careers in life have been in the theatre, education, local government, trade unionism and now, the hospitality game, you will appreciate that since all of those activities have a degree of mania about them probably a lot of damage was done!

Why do I talk about an Anderson shelter and what is the title of this talk? Well, the talk in its entirety is called "The Hazards of the Boards". 'The boards' is a euphemism for live theatre, so, the hazards of the boards are the things that go wrong if you tread the boards, i.e., perform in live theatre. Working in the theatre is a tricky enough game under any circumstances but, if it's live theatre, when things go wrong you have to just press on — there's nothing much else you can do and certainly, no one is going to say "cut". When the war was over, the air-raid shelter was dug up from my grandparents' garden and it was put back up, above-ground, in my father's garden. My father reckoned that he would make his fortune growing mushrooms in it. Unfortunately, the mushrooms had other ideas, so for some of the time the little air-raid shelter — now a corrugated shed, was used as a garage, but only part of the time, because my father quite often couldn't actually afford to run a car and even when he could, the cars that he owned were pretty cranky and would warrant a comic story all of their own. So, the little shed was partly redundant and therefore I was allowed to have it as my theatre. My career as an entrepreneur and performer in the theatre was guaranteed. If you are embarking on any production, having a venue is the first thing you have to sort out and now I had a ready-made venue — you have to remember, as I continue this tale, that I was at the time about six. I used to organise little concerts and my parents, my relations or my friends and their parents used to be inveigled into coming to the little concerts and were gracious enough to do so.

A regular member of my cast — often the only member of my cast, was my friend Jean. Yes, she was called Jean and I was called Jean. On one occasion, I was sorting out a little concert and I decided that the time had come to include in our programme a tap dance to a song. We'd not done that before. My friend Jean protested that she didn't know any songs and that she couldn't tap dance. Now my relationship with Jean was pretty straightforward, I led, and she followed, so I protested even louder that everybody knew some songs and I would teach her to tap dance. And so, it was. I put together a little collection of steps which fitted the tune of the one song she finally admitted that she knew, a song she had learned at school. I didn't know the song at all, she and I did not go to the same school. When I heard her sing it, I was delighted, as it was a perfect song for a tap dance. The great day came, the concert began, and Jean and I sang the song and did the dance to that remarkable piece of musical theatre music:

And did those feet in ancient time,
Walk upon England's mountains green?

The audience thought it was hilarious. I wasn't so sure that it was hilarious and didn't know why they thought it was funny. Someone soon enlightened me that it was not appropriate to do a song and dance act to 'Jerusalem'. I had goofed. But, you know, I hadn't. I was teased for that mistake for not just weeks, not just months, not just years, *decades*! I was only rescued when Russell Watson opened the Classical BRIT Awards at the Albert Hall singing 'Jerusalem' with not just the two Jeans, dancing in the background, but a whole bevvy of beautiful maidens. I had not committed a solecism, I had displayed prescience, although I have to admit that at the age of six, I didn't know what the word prescient meant and at the age of nearly eighty, I'm not actually sure that I can spell it! Thank you for listening. I'll tell you more stories of *The Hazards of the Boards* on another day.

2. Wands and Ringlets

Dancing schoolteachers are tyrants. You may not want to believe that, but I assure you it's true. I expect producers of musicals are tyrants as well, so that would include me. I learned the truth about dancing schoolteachers at a very early age. The instruction went out: "The concert is on Saturday and all fairies need a wand for the rehearsal on Thursday prior to the concert on Saturday." Fortunately, my grandad, the same one that dropped me, was very good at making things and, between whatever the day was that the announcement was given and the said Thursday, he made me an absolutely splendid wand, very beautiful, very sparkly. I was very proud of it, and I took it to my dancing school rehearsal convinced that my dancing schoolteacher would think it was splendid and she did — too splendid for an also-ran chorus fairy.

"Oh! Jean," she said, "what a lovely wand; much too good for the chorus, this must go to the fairy queen." I was divested of my wand instantly and given the fairy queen's, which not only was smaller than mine and not as sparkly as mine, but also, it also had the terrible deficiency that it drooped!

Now, if you think that's bad, the worst was still to come. That summer the dancing schoolteacher decided we would all take part in the local carnival; we would have a dancing school float and the theme of the float would be *The Wedding of the Painted Doll*. Her very favourite pupil was chosen to be the young bride and her very favourite male pupil — in fact, the only male pupil, in fact, her son — was chosen to be the bridegroom. All the rest of us, those that had been deemed also-ran chorus fairies, were now also-ran bridesmaids. The decree this time was, "All bridesmaids will have ringlets." Now, my hair is very fine and not given to curl — the slightest bit of wave on a good day but that's about it; enter my mother's friend, my mother's friend that always knew. It didn't matter what the problem was, she always knew. You've probably got a friend like that; nearly all of us have.

She said to my mother, "The solution is simple, you must put her hair in rags."

Now, if you've never had rags, you will not realise that these are a secret implement of female child torture. The hair is wound on little bits of cloth so that the head is covered with what appears to be little knots and then adults tell you big fibs and say, "Don't worry, when you go to bed you won't feel a thing." That's not true; they hurt, they're not very nice at all, but I duly endured a night of my hair being in rags and the next morning the rags were solemnly removed to reveal the ringlets. At least that was the plan, what actually happened was that my hair was as straight as it had ever been, and the floor was covered in beautiful little ringlets of rag. Why? Well, my mother had never had it pointed out to her that it mattered whether you wound the hair round rag or the rag around the hair and, whichever way it should have been, she'd done it the wrong way around. But never mind, being a sensible woman, she had given enough time, between this trial of acquiring ringlets and the actual event, for me to endure a second night of hair in rags, which was again pretty unpleasant. The next morning, however, triumph! Well not quite — there were curls — more like little corkscrews than ringlets but at least they were kinky — for at least ten minutes. By the time I was up and dressed, had eaten my cornflakes and was ready to go to school, my hair was pretty much as straight as it always is. Disaster? No! My mother's friend had another solution.

The other solution being curling tongs, and we're talking about 1948-ish curling tongs. They were like instruments of medieval torture. You got them red-hot in the bare flame on the gas stove and then you put the hair between the tong and the bit that clamps, and the idea was you would end up with curls.

My mother said, in my defence, "I can't use something like that on Jean's hair; it's much too fine, it will burn."

"Not so!" said my mother's friend. "You use lavatory paper between the tongs and the hair in order to act as a cushion."

So, this is what was done. Unfortunately, the lavatory paper of choice — and heaven knows whose choice it was in our household, was that stuff that's only any use if you're given tracing homework from school. Yes, you've guessed it… I don't know whether you can still buy it today. The next day when this awful experience occurred, the kitchen floor was soon covered with little bits of burnt or scorched loo roll and little bits of singed hair. The pong was alarming, and I looked like a scarecrow. My grandfather came to the rescue. Grandad took me to his hairdresser — a barber — quite a 'with it' barber because he offered a choice of style — you could have parting on the left, parting on the right, or, if you were really trendy, a parting down the middle. I came home with a haircut that was at least tidy.

My dancing schoolteacher, when she saw it, was appalled but she did have the grace to admit that an effort had been made to comply with her instruction for ringlets.

She said, "Well, I suppose, on the day, you'll have to wear a floral garland and we'll put up with it."

What she didn't know was that nearly every disaster has a silver lining. My silver lining was going to be brought about by the disaster of the fiery hairdressing and that will be my next story. Bye-bye.

3. The Hero of the Hour

Hello, it's me again. I'm back with the end of the tale I started to tell yesterday. I wasn't looking forward to the carnival procession with *The Wedding of the Painted Doll*. The float looked very nice, the costumes for the bride and the bridesmaids were pretty, even the little headdresses we'd been given to wear seemed to be fine, not, I'm pleased to say made by my grandfather, and all the same. However, mine did not do very much to disguise the fact that far from ringlets, my hairstyle was short back and sides.

However, little was I to know at the beginning of that day, that what started off for me as something I wasn't expecting much fun from, ended up bringing a delightful surprise, well delightful for me. We were getting ready to go; we were about to get dressed, to get onto the float when the news reached us. Disaster! The young man that was to be the bridegroom was ill, he had what is politely referred to as an upset stomach and what more accurately, but not so charmingly, is sometimes referred to as 'the runs'. Not a desirable condition if you are about to embark on a one and a half to two-hour ride on the back of a carnival float. What was going to happen? How could we have *The Wedding of the Painted Doll* without a bridegroom? My dancing teacher had the solution. She arrived minus son but armed with his costume, a smart little suit with a bow tie, etc. and who was it going to fit? Me! In those days, I was tall for my age, actually skinny and sporting the short back and sides to which we have referred. It fitted beautifully I am told, I looked very good in it. Miraculously I went, in the twinkling of an eye, from anonymous back-row bridesmaid to the hero of the hour. I was the bridegroom on the float and my gosh I enjoyed it! I didn't have to do very much, I just had to look sort of manly, fairly tricky when you're a young girl, but never mind, I managed it.

Little did I know the glory was not going to end there. In the crowds watching the carnival, it transpired, was the man who ran the local taxi firm. As he saw the wedding float, he thought he could use some of the ideas there to promote his wedding taxi service. So, shortly after the event, he arrived at my house having got my name and address from the dancing school, armed with a little document which he wished to discuss with me and my parents and for us the sign. It was a contract, a contract for my first paid engagement, hardly treading the boards riding in the back of a taxi, but related. For every Saturday of that summer, I in my little suit, with his daughter, who was the bride, of similar age to myself, rode in a ribbon-bedecked taxi around the town. The taxi sported labels and posters on the outside, advising that the firm could be used to enhance anyone's wedding. What's more, besides the glory, I received financial remuneration, a very small amount by our standards these days, but to me, as a young girl, it was the beginnings of a fortune. There was just one slight snag, my contract had a caveat, which was that under no circumstances should the bride, his daughter, become aware that the bridegroom, me, was actually a girl.

There is an epilogue to this story because shortly after these events, a whole crowd of us moved to the local secondary school. At the secondary school, in our English lessons, there was a set book to read, the set book: *Treasure Island*. What was my name in real life? Jean Hawkins and the hero of *Treasure Island* is Jim Hawkins, always called 'Jim Lad' by Long John Silver. Many of the girls who were in my class knew about the painted-doll saga and me being the bridegroom, so from that moment on, I was referred to as... Yes! you've guessed it... 'Jim Lad'. The nickname 'Jim Lad' stayed with me for all of the years I was at Chatham Girls Grammar School and many years after. When I was in the sixth form, I was still occasionally referred to as 'Jim Lad' by people who had no idea at all how that nickname had been conferred upon me. I look forward to talking to you tomorrow, to tell you about another of the hazards of the boards I've experienced in my interesting life treading the said boards. Bye-bye.

4. Leading Man and Leading Lady

Hello. To continue my tale, for seven years I was a pupil of Chatham Girls Grammar School. Chatham is one of the Medway towns. If you go to Kent and you drive through the Medway towns, Chatham, Gillingham, Rochester and various other smaller towns, you never have any idea when you are going from one to the other. If you live there, it's very important. Well, most certainly it was when I lived there and we're talking about the 1950s. Why should it be important? Well, each of the towns had an individual image; Rochester was, and probably still is, considered posh! Rochester had a cathedral, Rochester had a castle, Rochester had connotations with Dickens... all in all, the people in the Medway towns who considered themselves 'one above' lived in Rochester. Chatham was famous, as I've already mentioned, because it was a dockyard town, very busy, very bustling, and I lived in Chatham. Gillingham, what did Gillingham have? Well, it had one dancing school, which was the dancing school that I attended but it also had a Third Division football team. I think it still has a Third Division football team. Believe me, it mattered which of the towns you were in depending on what you were doing. I had lots of opportunity during my years at Chatham Girls Grammar School to indulge in all the things that I like to do. I had opportunities to sing, I had opportunities to continue to dance, and I had lots of opportunities to perform in and produce plays and suchlike, but I did encounter some hazards. One of the first major singing engagements I ever had was in Rochester Cathedral. I was chosen to sing the Christmas recitatives from *The Messiah*. I was very proud about this; I would have been about fourteen probably. I hope the local reporter who wrote up the event in the local paper couldn't actually see me from where he was sitting because the report read, "…the boy treble sang with a clear bell-like quality". Well, I was pleased about the 'clear bell-like quality' but not over enthusiastic about being described as the 'boy treble'.

Then there was the hazard, when performing in somewhere like the cathedral, as to what to wear. On one such occasion I was due to sing with the choir and my cousin Brenda, same sort of age as myself, was due to play in the orchestra. For once we were not expected to wear school uniform and we were given some money from each of our parents to go and buy ourselves a suitable dress for the event, a suitable black dress — and, of course, I mean one dress each not one between us. I chose my black dress quite quickly, I liked it, I could afford it, and I bought it. We went round shop after shop looking for a dress for my cousin. In the last shop a rather sniffy vendeuse produced one garment after another, all elegant black dresses, until my cousin Brenda cried out in exasperation, "They're none of them any good — they've all got straight skirts and I have to keep my legs apart!" She had failed to mention that she played the cello.

For all of the parts that I did in school productions I was grateful, I really couldn't complain. I did some extremely important and significant parts. Just one snag: they were all male. The school, after all, was Chatham Girls Grammar School. I was tall, I was skinny, I could lower the pitch of my voice if I wished to do so, and I was doomed to be a fella. The only pantomime I have ever been in was while I was at school, and I desperately wanted to have a good part. On that occasion I actually wanted to be a fella, there's a certain *je ne sais quoi* about being the Principal Boy — short velvet tunic, knee-high boots, long legs in tights... but no way. I wasn't cast as the Principal Boy, but I did get a female role. I was the Wicked Witch.

So, moving on, we arrive at the moment when I am in the sixth form, and I got probably the most symbolic role in straight drama that I have ever had. I was very proud, but what was the part? Well, it was a girl! How wonderful — I was going to be a girl — yes but what girl? Saint Joan! I spent the whole of that production dressed in hand-knitted chain mail made of garden string which had been dyed grey and then painted with aluminium paint. Not only did it itch appallingly, it also ponged alarmingly. However, the part is very dramatic especially the end. I don't know about you, but I have never watched the film *Titanic*. I won't watch *Titanic* because, of course, I know how it ends. And so it is with Saint Joan, we know how it ends. It ends with Joan tied to a funeral pyre burning at the stake. Now, my all-girls school did have a good science department and one of the staff came up with the idea that she would use lycopodium powder on a metal plate through which an electric current ran, as when warmed, lycopodium powder gives off a dense white smoke which is lighter than air and therefore rises. This device was manufactured and hidden on the set in the funeral pyre and at the right moment, when Joan looks towards the heavens and prays to her God, the white smoke went up around me. I tried to look suitably anguished, angelic and saintly, all at the same time. Not entirely easy when you're dressed in string and aluminium paint that pongs.

The scene went very well, it was most affecting, everyone said so, that is, right up until the last night. Picture the scene, I am on the stage, I am lashed to the funeral pyre, various of the rest of the cast are round grieving or gloating depending on which side they are on, and the fire starts to burn. Yes, well, some idiot had left a door open backstage. The front row of the audience on that night was the great and good of the Medway towns, and that's a lot of great and good, because it wasn't *one* mayor or *one* high sheriff, it was *three* mayors, *three* groups of officials, the Commandant of the Dockyard, the Dean of the Cathedral and the manager of the football team, etc. not to mention the school governors… all sitting in a long and erstwhile dignified front row. When the moment of Joan's death knell was tolled not one wisp of smoke went anywhere near me, it was the front row that died, asphyxiated by lycopodium powder smoke. I exaggerate of course; nobody actually died but there was an awful lot of coughing and spluttering, the end of the evening was not as dramatic as planned, melodramatic perhaps, but not dramatic.

I'll tell you some more stories on another occasion. Keep well, keep happy, keep safe and I'll try to keep you entertained. Bye-bye.

5. Take Your Seats — One

Hello. If there are noises off today different from the noises off on another day it's because I'm in the garden and the sun is shining and the birds are singing. The noises off in an earlier little missive from me were those of Peter, my husband, washing up rather loudly in the kitchen. Aspiring actors are often warned not to perform with children or animals. It's not because children or animals are necessarily difficult to perform with, it's because those who are good are really very good and tend to steal every scene they're in. I personally haven't experienced many problems performing with children or animals, though there was an occasion when the dog playing Sandy in *Annie* was in real life completely zany and manic. However, when the dog was introduced to the young lady playing Annie it was love at first sight on the dog's part and anything Annie wanted, the dog would do without any problems at all. Unfortunately, this good behaviour did not extend to the dressing room and one of the men in the chorus of that show complained officially to me and to my husband, the company manager, that someone in the cast had stolen his towel, a personalised towel that his sister had given him for a present. We expressed disappointment that this had occurred but didn't tell him that no one was guilty of stealing his towel — the dog had eaten it!

On another occasion a child did actually pose, momentarily, a slight problem. The small girl playing Gretel in *The Sound of Music* was the actual age that Gretel is meant to be, about six and a half, cute as can be and bright as a button. We were rehearsing the very complicated version of 'Do-re-mi' that the von Trapp family sings in the Salzburg Festival; it's winning that prize that enables them to escape from the Nazis at the awards ceremony. Well, we'd come to the end of our rehearsal of the piece, and it had gone reasonably well, when the small girl put up her hand and said to me, "Jean, someone behind me is singing this all wrong." At which point, the gentleman playing von Trapp hid his head in his hands. She was right, he had been singing it 'all wrong'.

My personal hazards on stage have been more with furniture than children or animals and that's going to be the focus of the stories I'm going to tell you this afternoon. A long time ago, I played Maria von Trapp in a production of *The Sound of Music,* and we had arrived in the show, an actual performance you understand, at the scene where Maria is about to teach all of the von Trapp children the *Do-re-mi* song. There was a velvet chaise longue on the stage where Maria was to sit with her guitar with the children grouped artistically on the floor or behind her and around her. To this day, the only chords I can play on a guitar are the ones which open 'Do-re-mi'. Just before the point of getting into this set-piece position, I was a bit taken aback when the scene, which had been going very well, had an unexpected visitor to the set, the chap playing Franz the butler. He walked in solemnly carrying a silver salver on which there was a small, folded note and I thought to myself, *why is Franz the butler approaching me; he is not in this scene?*

He bowed slightly and said solemnly, "Fraulein Maria," at which point I picked up the little note, opened the piece of paper and read what it said. It was very succinct and to the point — it said, 'Do not sit on the chaise as the back leg has just broken off!'

Well, what do you do? If you're on stage on your own it is simple to cover up something like that — go and sit somewhere else on the stage — but I wasn't on my own, I was accompanied by seven young people who would not have seen the contents of the note. Fortunately, part of the set was the end of a supposedly big grand staircase, and the bottom step was wide. I thought, if I go across and sit on the middle of the bottom step, the children can arrange themselves around me, as they would have done round the chaise. So that's fine, a good plan, except that I had no way of telling the children that this is what I wanted them to do. When I started to head 'stage right', when they were expecting me to go slightly 'left of centre' they must have all thought that I had gone completely nuts. However. The oldest of the von Trapp boys saved this particular day, because he had enough faith in me to appreciate that I wouldn't be going in the wrong direction just on a whim and he managed to shepherd all the rest of the children into place around the bottom of the steps. So, we got over that little hazard.

6. Take Your Seats — Two

A year later, a different show, therefore, a different part, a different theatre, but the same theatre company and the same furniture. That chaise was going to haunt me again. The show in question this time was *The Merry Widow,* and I had the great pleasure of playing Anna Glavari, the widow. I'm not a great one for favourites but if I were pushed to give my favourite opera or musical, I think *The Merry Widow* would be a very strong contender for the top spot. It's got a plausible story, lots of nice parts, splendid costumes and Franz Lehar's most beautiful romantic music. Basically, the story is about an aristocrat, Count Danilo Danilovich and a girl, Anna. They were in love years ago, but his aristocratic parents wouldn't let him pursue a relationship with a peasant girl. At the time the musical starts, Anna is no longer a peasant girl, she is a lady of society, recently widowed and very, very wealthy. Danilo, still a bachelor, is part of the diplomatic corps of Pontevedro, a made-up European state and Pontevedro is going bust. Danilo is convinced by his superiors that he must woo and wed the widow or Pontevedro will be bankrupt. I tell you this because it sets the scene for the disaster, or near disaster, that unbeknownst to us was about to occur.

Imagine the last moments of Act One: the lovers, although they're much too proud to admit to each other that they still love each other, are alone on the stage singing and waltzing and the scene about to end in the inevitable rose-lit clinch. I was playing Anna and I had a beautiful Edwardian evening dress, velvet with a built-in train in the skirt, made as it would have been authentically, the hem of the train had little weights in it. That's done so that when you wear a dress like that, and you walk along and turn around, the dress smoothly comes round behind you and doesn't end up looking like a duvet on the morning after you've had a very bad night. On the stage, of course, was the chaise longue; it had not only been repaired since the last tale I told you about it, but it had been refurbished and now each of the legs, very secure legs, ended in a brass ferrule, and the brass ferrule has within it a caster, which is how it would have been originally. The stage on which we were performing was a raked stage — that means that the stage sloped slightly from front up towards the back. No one had had any hazard with the chaise during the whole of the first act: people had sat on it, I had sat on it; people had embraced on it, I hadn't embraced on it, no problem. So, the waltz begins.

Now, if you've ever danced in an Edwardian evening dress, you will know that usually there is a loop sewn to the seam of the train, and that as you dance, you can put the loop over your wrist and lift the train out of the way, so that you don't trip over it in an undignified manner. This is how the dance began, and all was well. There we were, Danilo and I, looking at each other as though we were passionately in love, singing away, dancing away, keeping an eye on the conductor — not entirely easy to do all of those things at once, but we were managing it, until the loop that was attached to my dress suddenly decided to become unattached. My grandmother would have said that whoever sewed the loop on did so with red-hot cotton. I continued to waltz; the train spread out behind me, and I think it looked very beautiful, until the train caught the caster on one of the legs of the chaise, which began a slow but inexorable movement forward down the slightly sloping stage. In front of the stage is a very deep orchestra pit and the consequences of the chaise going straight down towards the orchestra could have been quite dangerous, if not disastrous. However, the chaise's progress was hampered because the caster caught the bottom of a flat. Stage flats are about four feet wide and about sixteen to twenty feet high and I suppose if you're going to have anything land on top of you, you could imagine a lot worse, because usually they consist of a wooden frame filled in with canvas and if you knock a flat over, it falls slowly. It falls slowly because the canvas has a slight parachute effect as the whole thing falls forward. The chaise catches the bottom of the flat, the flat starts to teeter and then it starts to fall. Every single person in the theatre knew what was happening except the chap playing Danilo and me. We were so busy trying to cope with all the things that were part of our official role that neither of us had the faintest idea that any such accident was going to happen. We got to the end of the song; we're in the centre of the stage; the lights have changed into a romantic pink hue. 'We're about to have the final clinch and the curtain is about to fall, when the stage manager — this time he was the hero of the hour, came pounding across from the side of the stage to just behind us, lifted one hand aloft and caught the wooden edge of the frame just before the whole flat was about to land on our heads. The curtain came down at that precise moment and the audience erupted into tremendous applause; none of it was for me. Thank you for listening, I'll tell you some more another day. Bye-bye.

7. Mozart's Pantomime

Hello, I've come back to tell you another story. From the moment that I first went to dancing school, aged four, and first trod the boards, I was sunk, hook, line and sinker; love at first sight. I was utterly convinced throughout nearly all of my school years that the theatre, in some form or other, would be my livelihood. In fact, it never was, and why was that? Because of another hazard! There was to be a gala concert in The Chatham Empire to raise money for a disaster to a submarine. Representing the dancing school, I and the young man who was my partner were going to dance a formal pas de deux from one of the classical ballets. In the event, we never did, because at the rehearsal he dropped me. Not intentionally you understand, and it may have been my fault. Perhaps I jumped too soon, perhaps he wasn't looking; perhaps we were out of time with the music — whatever, it doesn't matter. The result of the crash was that I damaged my ankle, not so severely as to be permanent, but badly enough to mean that for some weeks, or months, I wasn't going to be concentrating on dance and the theatre. It so happened that this accident occurred just before I was due to sit the exams that in those days were 'O levels', so I got stuck into my schoolwork and to my amazement I discovered that actually I liked things academic. Even more surprisingly, I was good at them! All this just before I went into the sixth form and had to start thinking about what I was going to do at university. I changed my mind entirely, and, casting aside my theatrical ambitions, I went to university to read for an Honours degree in maths and physics. Everybody was amazed. Everybody, that is, apart from my mother's always-knowing friend who was heard to say, "I don't know why everyone should be so surprised that Jean is doing physics, she's always been very physical."

I, over the years, have directed, performed in, choreographed, stage-managed, crewed so many shows, musicals, operas and occasional straight plays that I have completely lost count of how many. It's been a joy, and it's been a great pleasure to me to have, what might be called, a second string to my bow. If you've been struggling all day with a class of teenagers, trying to inveigle them into understanding, for instance, the refraction of light through glass prisms — or if you've been all day struggling with directives from the DfE or the DES or whatever particular set of initials the Education Department is using at the time — you cannot go home and fret about such tribulations if, in the evening you've got thirty people in front of you who've mostly got two left feet and you've got to teach them all a dance. A different focus is a wonderful way of relaxing if you're not very good at just collapsing on a sofa with a book — and I've never been very good at that until, perhaps, now. I'm better at it now. Of all the shows that I've done, most of them I'm happy to say have been successful and I've been pleased with what I had produced, or performed in, or choreographed, so it's rather odd that it's the ones where things went wrong that stick in the memory and I'm going to tell you about two of those, one now and then I'll tell you about the other one tomorrow.

There are two shows that I have directed where I could, and sometimes have, devoted a whole talk to the 'disasters', in inverted commas, that occurred during the productions. 'Disasters' which at the time seemed mortifying and upon reflection now seem very funny. The first one concerns *The Magic Flute*. Mozart wrote *The Magic Flute* as his last opera, and it was written to entertain a club. Some people have called it Mozart's pantomime. It certainly has an eclectic mixture of characters and a rather convoluted story. When I directed *The Magic Flute*, there were more women in the company than there were men, and the chorus music is written for mostly men. Our musical director modified the chorus music so that a four-part mixed chorus could sing it. One of the things that I had a hand in, was choosing the sort of costumes that people would wear, bearing in mind that the chorus was going to be men and women of various ages and sizes and I wanted them all to be dressed the same. I, with the help of the wardrobe mistress, put together a costume which consisted of black knee breeches, a black tunic, a coloured sash and matching turban, white tights and buckled shoes. Everyone could wear this outfit, and all felt comfortable with the design and so the wardrobe mistress set about making the costumes as rehearsals proceeded.

In *The Magic Flute*, there is a character called Papageno, the bird catcher, and he sings about catching birds. I arranged that while he was singing his song, a group of six teenage girls would dance as birds. They would mimic the movements of birds, hopefully in an elegant and attractive way, while he sang. Now at that time, we had a gentleman called Archie, who always made the props for the productions. A very taciturn gentleman but very good at making props. I went to him and said that there was a bird-catcher in the show and could he possibly make a birdcage for the bird-catcher. He said that he would. When we arrived at the first technical run-through, the birdcage appeared. However, before I saw it, Archie said, "I did your birdcage, but they won't all get in it!"

When I looked, I was amazed and appalled, the birdcage was enormous, and why was it enormous? Archie came every week to make the tea and had seen the group of six teenage girls rehearsing the bird dance, so he had made a cage for teenage girl size 'birds' to be enclosed within. I drew breath with horror and thought, *Oh, my goodness what am I going to do?* I didn't think the girls themselves would be very keen on being asked to spend a good deal of the show in a cage, but we couldn't *not* use the cage, as the poor man would be so unhappy, so hurt.

So, I said to him, "Archie, your cage is magnificent; could you make a small replica for Papageno to actually carry?"

"Yes," he said, "if you like."

I sent out an urgent SOS that very night to the company, saying that if any of them had small children who would like to be in the show as little baby birds, then that would be very helpful and attractive. The wardrobe mistress looked a bit aghast knowing that the next request was going to be, could she make baby bird costumes ASAP, which she did. I heaved a sigh of relief and though it was at very short notice, the birdcage problem was solved. Having baby birds on board was no bad thing because, whenever small children are in a show, it always sells extra tickets

Then we get to the first dress rehearsal in costume and all of the company arrived on stage in their little uniforms, black breeches, black tunics, coloured sashes, coloured turbans. The wardrobe mistress had chosen different coloured sashes and turbans for each member of the chorus so that the whole thing looked brighter and more cheerful. She had chosen a particular orange, a particular luminous pink, a particular white, a particular brownish colour and a particular turquoise colour. I stood at the back of the auditorium and looked in horror at what I had generated on the stage: a whole chorus of Liquorice Allsorts Bertie Bassett men. I didn't say a word. I *couldn't* say anything, but I hoped that nobody else noticed that they all looked exactly like the illustrations at that time on the packets of Liquorice Allsorts. In my horror, I hoped that nothing else was going to go wrong.

Now there is an entrance of the priests in *The Magic Flute* and the particular piece of music is very 'limpy' music, it has a sort to bounce to it. There is a chief priest who is a tenor and a chief priest who is a baritone. I had cast two men for these two parts because they had excellent voices, but, as it happened, both of them limped. One limped because as a child he'd had polio and one limped because as a young man he'd been in a motorbike accident. When it came to the moment of the arrival of the priests, one team of priests entered from one side and one team of priests entered from the other. To my horror the chief priests limped in mirror image of each other. Standing next to me at the back of the auditorium was a critic who at that time used to write for the local newspaper and he muttered, "Ah! An initiation procedure?"

I had no idea what he was talking about until, many years afterwards, I watched an episode of *Midsomer Murders*, where the trusty sergeant joined the Freemasons to help solve a crime and had to go through a Freemasons initiation ceremony with his trouser legs rolled up to his knees, one foot incapacitated by the removal of a shoe and a pebble in the other shoe, so that he arrived limping. I had inadvertently displayed the same prescience, without knowing it, as I had done many years ago, because it wasn't an accident that the music was 'limpy', Mozart was a freemason. I thought I got away with it all, particularly the costumes, until the next time I directed *The Magic Flute*.

I was trying to sell some tickets to a friend, and he said, "Oh yes! I saw your earlier *Magic Flute*, the definitive Bertie Bassett Freemason version."

Bye-bye.

8. Be Careful What You Wish For

The first time I ever did a talk to a Women's Institute, the topic that they asked me to speak to was, 'How I got to be where I am today'.

When I thought about it, the answer was very simple: the number 8 bus, but of course that wasn't what they meant. When you ask a question, you have to be very sure that you're going to get the answer that you want. On one occasion, when I was invigilating an exam in my education days, I read a question on an exam paper which said, *Many light industries in the East Midlands employ women in part-time capacities. Name three of them.* I read the beginning of one young man's answer to that question. He had written, "Enid, Joan and Margaret. I know this answer is correct because Enid is my mother and Joan, and Margaret are her friends. That's not really what you want to know…" And he then proceeded to write a very good essay about light industry in the East Midlands. Why do I tell you this story? Because the title of this last section of *The Hazards of the Boards* is, *Be Careful What You Wish For.*

My early excursions into playing parts in Shakespeare productions were not overly auspicious. On the first occasion, I had very few words but a splendid costume with the most beautiful back, which was all the audience saw for most of the time. I was playing Cobweb in *A Midsummer Night's Dream*; I was in my first year at secondary school and the art teacher had made a sort of little cape for my costume which fastened on my shoulders and then down to my wrists and had the most beautiful cobweb embroidered upon it, hence I spent most of that performance with my back to the audience. By the time I was in the second year, the school Shakespeare play was *As You Like It* and my part, was to be one of the pages who sings 'There was a lover and his lass'. I wore a little doublet and hose made of a fabric with half-inch wide stripes in white and Barbie-doll pink. I was also given a little aide-memoire.

My uncle, my dad's brother, found this little aide-memoire, picked it up, read it and said, "What's this Jean?"

I replied, "Oh it's my part in the school play". With a big grin on his face, he read out, "log on — log off — log on — log off—" and I had to explain to him that we were performing on the school stage which wasn't very big and there wasn't much scenery, and that half of the play is set in the Forest of Arden and half of the play is set in the Court.

"When the scene is the Forest of Arden, I and the other page bring on a log and when the scene is the Court, we take the log off."

He wasn't overly complimentary about that particular part of my responsibility. When he came to see the show nothing at all was said about my singing, he was just amused at my efforts with the log and it's the log that features in this last story.

There is an operetta called *The Great Waltz*; it's about Strauss the Elder and his rivalry with his own son, Strauss the Younger, it is in fact true that they were rivals- and also about a liaison between Strauss the Elder and a prima donna opera singer, which I think is probably fiction. There is one scene in the show where the opera singer appears in the Vienna Woods regaled in a beautiful red lace crinoline ball gown and sits on a log and sings an aria set to some of Strauss' music. Of course, it's not overly usual to wear a ball gown when walking in the Vienna Woods, but who am I to complain? At the dress rehearsal, the said prima donna arrived elegantly and sat down, with some difficulty, on the log. It was a perfectly sound and substantial log, but it was very small and if you've ever been to a school nativity play and had to aim for the tiny seat that is provided for you to watch the show, you will know the difficulty that she might have encountered; however, she sang beautifully. When the rehearsal was over, I said to the young man in charge of props, "Would it be possible, before tomorrow, to find a rather bigger log for the opera singer to sit on so that her descent, as it were, is less precarious?"

He said he would do his best. We come to the first night and there on the stage is a very respectable substantial log, roughly dining chair height. The prima donna appears, sits down and again sings beautifully. She then gets up to graciously exit from the stage. Her dress was made of red nylon tulle; the log, unfortunately, was made of polystyrene and very light in weight, so the static electricity generated between these two synthetic materials was such that, as the prima donna swept from the stage, she did so with the log firmly attached to her backside! The audience, of course, thought it was hilarious. I happened to be standing near the props man in the wings, who grabbed my arm saying, "She'll kill me, she'll kill me!"

Only then did I appreciate that the props chap was the son of the woman singing the soprano role. He did his mother an injustice — she was a true star and did the only thing she could do — she joined in the laughter.

In a later scene in the operetta, the prima donna is again on stage, again in her beautiful lace crinoline and she has to drop a handkerchief provocatively. Strauss the Elder picks it up, hands it back to her, their eyes meet — and they have 'a moment'. Well, that's what happened at the dress rehearsal except that actually no handkerchief was involved because it had been inadvertently left in the dressing room, so they mimed the little incident and did it beautifully. Now there is a lace handkerchief, there is a crinoline, which is a very sticking-out crinoline, and the soprano in question was small of stature and therefore had fairly short arms. When she stretched out her arm and gracefully dropped the handkerchief, the handkerchief floated down beautifully — onto the crinoline skirt where it adhered firmly just as the log had done. The actor playing Strauss the Elder looked for it on the ground to pick it up; he couldn't find it, so he moved around behind the lady. She started to look for it; even members of the audience started to join in helpfully calling out to explain that the handkerchief was not on the ground, it was on the skirt.

Eventually it was retrieved, and the Strauss the Elder character left the stage, somewhat nonplussed. He went straight to his dressing room and collapsed in a heap wondering what he had done to deserve all that. He'd only been sitting in his dressing room for a few seconds when to his dismay he heard the orchestra playing the introduction to the best song he had in the show and, realising that he should be on stage and not in his dressing room, he charged down the stairs and entered the stage through the first gap in the scenery that he encountered. It was now that the audience were somewhat nonplussed themselves when our hero entered the heroine's boudoir through the inglenook fireplace. That was not the end of the hazards encountered that night! Everything that could have gone wrong that night did. Fortunately, it was a '"one-night-only' going wrong, the next night and the rest of the run went without a hitch. All of the 'disasters' were sorted out and they had all occurred because I simply said, "Can I please have a log?"

I hope you've enjoyed *The Hazards of the Boards*. I shall enjoy doing another talk on another topic in the near future. Bye-bye!

Tribute And Promise

1. The Project Takes Off

Hello. A quarter of a century ago, I was invited by Peter Hilton, the then Lord Lieutenant of Derbyshire, to take a major part in staging an event that was going to be put on at the opera house in Buxton. The event was the brainchild of Peter and his wife Winifred and was to be called *Tribute and Promise*. It was to be a celebration of the 50th anniversary of the end of hostilities in Europe in the Second World War. That's the sort of invitation that you don't refuse. The plan for the evening was that one third of the proceedings would take the form of an Act of Remembrance and the other two-thirds would be a Celebratory Concert. There would be representatives of the Armed Forces present; there would be various members of the clergy; there would be, in the audience, many invited guests from both Derbyshire and other parts of the British Isles. It was to be a big do! Peter and Winifred were keen that the entertainment part would involve as many people as possible from the county of Derbyshire or thereabouts, who in any way performed: singers, dancers, musicians, you name it. My job was to be responsible entirely for the entertainment, but with an overview of all the staging within the theatre.

Well, to begin with, I had to gather together a massive cast, so I designed a form, which I didn't think was rocket science, and sent it to the secretaries of various local groups. The form had questions like: *What is the title of your group? What will be the nature of the item you could present at the concert? How long is it likely to take? How many people will be involved? Do you have your own transport? Will you need us to provide accompaniment, or will you have your own accompaniment?* and so on. The forms were duly sent out to all sorts of groups, and I waited in anticipation of their return. It didn't take long before the first one came back. I opened it and it was immaculately filled-in, looked beautifully neat and was very organised. At the top, *What is the name of your group?* Well, that was clearly stated and then the fun started. *What would be the nature of your item?* To be decided. *How many people will be involved in your part of the show?* Not yet known. *Will you need your own transport, or will you need help with transport?* See above. I presume that meant, *Also, not yet known* and so on, and so forth, until I arrived at a flourishing signature of the bottom of the page. Well, I knew two things, I knew the name of the group and I knew the name of the secretary thereof, but I knew nothing else whatsoever. Then another one came, and I opened that. This one looked a bit of a shambles, it had been filled in, I suspect, by the whole committee, each item appeared to be written, with a different writing implement, in different handwriting and (my gosh!), the amount of information was immense and amazing. It overtook all of the lines provided and went up and round the corners. As an artwork, it was quite fun, but it was no more informative really, than the first one, because for instance, *How many people in your group?* Answer: *Well, it will depend on whether or not Freda can come, because Freda's husband usually drives us, but he's been unwell, if it's Tom that drives us, well then, Maisie and Flo don't get on with Tom, so they might not be involved after all.* I am, of course, inventing the names, and so it went on. As a social document of the ins and outs of the intrigues and friendships of that group, it could probably have made interesting reading, but it didn't help me very much. But many of the forms that were returned were more coherent than that one. There was one form which was just wonderful: *What is the name of your group?* Clearly stated. *How many people will be involved?* Fifteen. *Will you have your own costumes?* Yes. *Will you provide your own transport?* Yes. *What is the length of your item?* Approximately four and a half minutes. And so on and so forth. And when it came to the day, everything was, as they say, 'Ronseal-wise', "As it said on the tin". I do not know what that group actually did on the stage; I didn't see their item. I do know that, at the end of the evening, they came and thanked me for all my help, when I actually wanted to throw my arms around the secretary and give her a hug, because she and her group had brought a degree of sanity to the organisation of the day, that otherwise, might not have been there. These days, the group probably has a more PC title, but in those days, I think they were called the 'League of Health and Beauty': ladies that wore sleeveless satin blouses, black Directoire knickers and swung Indian clubs, etc.

So, I had a cast, I had a very big cast, and a rehearsal was planned. Please note, a rehearsal was *planned*. Whenever there are very major events, involving a great many people, usually, you only get one rehearsal. I had invited my own singing group to perform as part of the entertainment and when it came to the rehearsal, I said to them that they didn't need to come to the whole of the rehearsal day, because I knew that they knew what they were doing, because we'd rehearsed it in our normal rehearsal time. Fat chance that was! They all turned up with their thermos flasks and their packed lunches and they all sat in the auditorium of Buxton Opera House all day, having a splendidly entertaining time, watching me outside my comfort zone. I had been allocated, for the day, a very splendid gentleman, whose uniform had a great deal of braid on it, referred to as my ADC (aide-de-camp). He was really my guide and mentor, to make sure that, whatever I did was according to appropriate military protocol.

One of the big parts of the whole thing, was a parade of the banners of the British Legion. Did I say banners? Should I have said flags? Should I have said standards? Yes indeed, I should have said standards. And when on the day, I got the word wrong, not once, but more than once, if looks could kill, I wouldn't be talking to you now. The standard bearers all arrived to practise and were, for the most part, persons of mature years. The standards are big and heavy, and the route from the auditorium up onto the stage at Buxton is steep. There are no permanent front stage steps, so a set of treads had been brought in for the occasion, but the treads were steep, and the treads had no banister rails. So, the first snag was getting my standard bearers to proceed up to the stage in the right order, at the right moment. I wondered, for a while, how that was going to be affected safely, but then it occurred to me that I had to hand a stalwart bunch of young men. In those days, they were all young men. What bunch? The Sea Cadets of Buxton. It's always puzzled me somewhat, why the most landlocked town in the British Isles has Sea Cadets, but it does, and they did a grand job, helping the standard bearers to safely move from the auditorium to the stage.

When they were on the stage, I grouped them into a tableau, which I thought looked attractive. That was fine, until my ADC tapped me on the shoulder and said,

"Excuse me Ma'am, very attractive to look at, but I fear, not according to protocol."

"Oh dear!" said I, "What's wrong?"

"Well," he said, "Ma'am, the Senior Service needs to be prominent."

The Senior Service is the Navy. Now, the Navy standard, not surprisingly, is navy blue. The Air Force standards are Air Force blue and many of them have beautiful silver wings and similar symbols embroidered upon them. The Army standards are so many, various and glorious, that they look as though they've come from the world of operetta, with lions and unicorns, crowns and tassels. I had made a splendid picture of the grouping of the standards, but now I had to decide how to change this, to make the Senior Service prominent. Then I realised that that involved everybody going back down to the auditorium, because they all had to come up in a different order, to form the new tableau. Well, with some difficulty, everyone reached the auditorium safely. There was a great deal of milling around and I said, "Stop, stop, stop! You've got to line up to come back." And absolutely nothing happened.

My aide said, quietly, "Excuse me, Ma'am. Try, Halt! As you were!"

So, I did, and they did. It's wonderful what speaking the right language, at the right time, can do. The new tableau looked pretty good, but the Senior Service, the Navy's, standard in the middle, at the front, became almost invisible, absolutely swamped by the glorious Technicolor of the rest of the standards. My aide said, "Oh, Ma'am, much better!"

Then I realised, he was an army man.

2. Happy Landings

There are very specific difficulties in coping with a very large cast. For a start, if all the performers turned up at once, where would one put them? The dressing rooms certainly couldn't cope with everybody at the same time and if the House is going to be pretty full, in terms of audience, then everybody altogether makes a big deal. There were many occasions in that rehearsal, when I inadvertently put my foot in it, usually, because I wasn't used to dealing with things pertaining to the Armed Forces or, for that matter, the Church. Most of the entertainment items went quite smoothly in rehearsal because the performers had had opportunity to rehearse their bits in their own places of practice. It was the occasions when everything had to be united that caused the problems, or the laughter. There was one wonderful moment, when we were rehearsing the Remembrance part of the evening, when I assumed that the young airman who was going to play the 'Last Post' on his cornet was right at the top of the opera house at the back of the gallery. I'm told I have a voice that could quell a riot at 200 yards, if necessary, and using that voice, I bawled across the theatre that we were ready for him to try the 'Last Post'. Whereupon, a very charming young airman standing to my left, leant forward and said, "Ma'am, I'm here!"

The people in the audience that were in my own company thought that was just wonderful. In fact, he never did get to practice the 'Last Post', because at that moment, the ominous sound of a big bass drum being played some distance away permeated the theatre.

Usually when there is a performance, the audience arrives in dribs and drabs, in the half an hour or so between the House opening and the show starting, but on this occasion, the plan was, that all the audience would gather in the Pavilion Gardens and they would be led in, in procession, by the various bands that were playing in the concert. You can hear bass sounds from a long way away and the bass drum that I could hear was indicative of the fact that the procession was getting ready to move towards the theatre. Rehearsal time was over. The show was about to start. There was a frantic tidying up of the stage, which was not easy, because there were orchestra stands and goodness knows what else in the way, and props everywhere. I suddenly realised that I was still wearing what I'd been wearing since the crack of dawn, a tracksuit type of garment, whose only virtue was comfort. At some point during the evening, I was supposed to make an appearance on stage. Fortunately, my husband Peter and I own a house that's near the theatre and my long-suffering fella was sent to find the evening dress that I had hung out in readiness to change, not having a clue that I wouldn't have time to go back home and change properly. People who've worked in the theatre, especially musical theatre, for years, think nothing much of changing in the wings. Composers have an unerring habit of assuming that one can change from one garment to another in four bars of music, and then, you're on again. So, I removed my tracksuit and put my evening dress on, in the wings, and only after I had successfully effected this change, did I glance up, and realise that the masking in the theatre on that day was not great, and that there was a perfect sight line, between where I was standing and the main box in the theatre, where Winifred Hilton was sitting next to, I think, the Archbishop of Westminster. Either they were both short-sighted, or they were both much too polite to register any sort of distress at what they might have seen. Either way, I got away with it.

You'll notice that I didn't say Sir Peter was in the box, that was because, though he had been one of the prime movers and shakers of the whole event, he sadly had died. For a while, we thought the event wouldn't happen, but indeed the opposite occurred, the title 'Tribute And Promise' applied to the way the people of Derbyshire felt about him and so, far from diminishing the occasion, he and his memory enhanced it.

It looked, therefore, as though we were going to be 'Up and running' and 'All will be well'. We were into the second half when my mentor tapped me on the shoulder and said, "Ma'am, the Colour Parties are at the Stage Door."

Not knowing what he meant by the 'Colour Parties', I said, "Oh?" and he said, "I think you should come," so I went to the Stage Door. In Water Street, which is next to the theatre, there were, what seemed like hundreds of people, probably thirty or so, of every size shape and uniform, milling around.

"The Colour Parties," my ADC said, "what do you want me to do with them?"

That was an unfortunate question, because I might have invented a less than gracious answer, and I said, "Oh, whatever they did this morning."

He said, "Well, they weren't here this morning." "Why not?" said I.

"Well, they weren't mustered," he said.

Yes, well they may not have been mustered, but they were supposed to be in the performance. Apparently, they were supposed to accompany the standards and, you will remember, we'd already had fun and games about getting the standard bearers from the auditorium to the stage and into the new tableau. At that point, I decided to let diplomacy fly to the wings, and I exercised a degree of authority, which I can do (I was head a very large comprehensive school for a lot of years).

I said, "Without any concession to size, status, affiliation, gender or rank, I want one line on this street now, from 'small to tall to small'. Go!"

You may not be familiar with the phrase, 'small to tall to small': it's a trick that choreographers and sergeant majors use, when they wish to give the impression of a straight line, where everyone is the same height. Of course, everyone is not the same height and if you want a line to look funny you muddle it up so the very tallest is next to the very shortest and the thinnest next to the fattest, etc. 'Small to tall to small', or sometimes, 'tall to small to tall', gives an impression of a continuity of height. If you ever watch the Trooping of the Colour, have a look. The uniformity that was achieved, in no time flat, was just astounding and my guide and mentor even chose to move a couple of people, as this was his ploy of being helpful. Now, when you do that, you have to pray that the smallest and the tallest are people with considerable nous and quick on the uptake and, in this situation, the two smallest, albeit uniformed, were Cub Scouts, aged about, perhaps seven.

I go to one of them and I say, "In a moment I will show you the way onto the back of the stage. You are to lead this line up the steps, onto the stage, across the back of the stage and you are to stop when you are level with the microphone that you will see protruding from the orchestra pit near the wings. Got that?"

The little boy looked at me and solemnly said, "Roger that Ma'am!" which I think meant "Yes"!

I then went to the tallest chap, who was a dead ringer for Ian Lavender; he didn't have a muffler on, and said, "You have to progress across the stage until you are level with the conductor, which will indicate you are in the centre of the stage, and you are to stay there."

I then, went to the other little boy, at the very far end, and said, "You will be the last onto the stage and you have got to get onto the stage and be opposite the microphone on your side of the orchestra pit, even if that means pushing the people in front of you."

I then addressed the whole group and said, "I know that 'dressing' is the way to get equal spaces, but there won't be room to do that, you will just have to shuffle a bit. I think that caused a look of pain to go across my ADC's face, but he was kind enough not to say anything. I took them to the steps at side stage and as the standard bearers were being helped up from the auditorium to make their tableau this long line walked across the back. In their ill-assorted uniforms, it looked splendid, and it was like having a screen behind the banner tableau. I heaved a sigh of relief and sent up a silent prayer of thanks. At which point my ADC tapped me on the shoulder and said, "Well done Ma'am!"

The whole event was well done. It was a fitting tribute to say, "Thank you".

Added for VE Day 2020

[Today is another occasion to say, "Thank you". We won't all be at Buxton Opera House, or in street party, but we can all say, "Thank you", in our hearts, in the difficult time that we're now in. And to echo, both Vera Lynn and the Queen, "We'll meet again". I shall come and talk to you again sometime. I hope you enjoyed listening.]

3. Another Promise — Devonshire 300

Hello. In 1994, the Duke of Devonshire commissioned a special work to be composed to celebrate a momentous occasion in the history of Chatsworth. The celebration was not such as we lesser mortals would celebrate, a birthday, a wedding anniversary, an engagement or a coming-of-age, it was to mark 300 years of the Dukedom. Very few of us are in a position to be able to celebrate that. I was lucky enough to be invited to be one of the people to help make this celebration work.

First of all, a pageant was written. Well, *I* would have called it a pageant, but the author who wrote it called it a 'masque'. It was the story of the Cavendish family from the point when they were ennobled as the Dukes of Devonshire to the present day. They were granted this great honour by way of a 'Thank you' for helping to get William and Mary safely and peacefully onto the throne of this country when we had, unfortunately, run out of monarchs. Next, everybody involved was gathered together for a preliminary meeting at Chatsworth and everybody was a lot of people. There were at least two hundred and fifty performers not to mention all of the technicians and other helpers that were involved. In overall charge, as I recollect, was one Freddie Meynell of the Meynell Hunt family, a small wiry man looking like and built like a jockey, who always wore jodhpurs and riding boots and carried in one hand a telephone about the size of a brick and in the other a riding crop. He was mercurial and ubiquitous, and he needed to be to keep all of that lot in order. There was a miracle to help him, for a whole week in May in Derbyshire, it didn't rain, it was pretty chilly, but it didn't rain. As I drove into the parkland on that first day, I could see in the distance what looked like a little red Lego structure. I realised that it was the stand erected for the audience. I remember thinking, *Well, we won't seat many people in that*, until I got nearer to it and found it was huge, plenty big enough to accommodate the size of audience anticipated, something around three thousand in total. It was the vastness of the Chatsworth Park that had diminished the structure into appearing like a toy when I had first seen it.

The plan was that the masque would be performed three times and consist of various scenes each of which would represent the life of a particular duke. The dukes were all to be played by professional actors. My duke was the 9th Duke, whose great interest in life was gambling and horse racing. Special music had been composed for the whole event and the music that I was going to use was very lively and very cheerful. It was great fun putting together a dance drama to give an impression of racegoers, jockeys and bookies sharing the excitement of a big race meeting. The first night invited audience was made up entirely of friends and relations of the cast. In a sense, that first night was a dress rehearsal. The next night was devoted to being a 'Thank you' given to all of the servants and retainers of the Devonshire households in Derbyshire, in London and their estates in the West Country and Ireland. Then, on the third night the masque was performed to a fee-paying audience with all of the money, and the tickets were a pretty hefty price, going to the Children's Society charity.

When it came to the first night, all went amazingly well. The audience filled the tiers of the seating, and they were thrilled to see a very large barge decked about like a royal barge with oarsmen: the Buxton Sea Cadets again, this time in fine livery. The boatman standing at the prow and at the stern, in regal attire, the figures of William and Mary. On the quay, newly erected out of scaffolding, were all of the actor 'Dukes of Devonshire 'grouped in a tableau waiting to greet the new King and Queen when they arrived and to swear the allegiance of the people of England, and in particular Derbyshire, to the new monarchs. So, the barge comes along, and the boatman gives the signal for the oarsmen to loft their oars which they do. Lofting the oars means that they are raised into a vertical position which in turn means that the oarsmen all get very wet with splattered water and have to then pretend that hasn't happened in order to maintain total dignity and solemnity. The boatman 'slings his hook', which is a phrase I'm sure you're all familiar with and hooks it onto the scaffolding of the quayside. Then he gently pulls the barge into the landing stage so that the royal couple can alight. Well, that's what should have happened and that's what did happen. The oarsmen then rowed the barge out of the lake and along the river until out of sight. And, to use a racing phrase, "We were off!" Now, if you have been involved in theatrical activities yourself, you will know that the dress rehearsal isn't always absolutely ready for the perfection of performance and our quasi-dress rehearsal was no different. Between the evening of the performance for friends and relatives and the evening of the first truly public showing, the set builders had very carefully turned the scaffolding quayside into something that looked remarkably similar to the stone of Chatsworth House. Visually very impressive and nobody appreciated at first the significance of this 'improvement'. So, the music starts, the audience claps in happy anticipation and the barge comes into view. The boat gets level with the quayside and the oarsmen is about to 'sling his hook' and there is nothing whatsoever to hook his hook onto, because the scaffolding is now covered by the fake stone. A river flows through the lake at Chatsworth and there is a quite powerful current, so the barge doesn't stop at the landing stage, even though the oarsmen are no longer rowing, but continues happily on its way. If William and Mary can't get off, there won't be a pageant! My duke, the 9th duke, standing there in splendid state in his fine outfit was, thank goodness, wide awake. He realised what was happening, dashed down towards the barge, and managed to get hold of the boatman's hook. The other dukes by then had woken up and joined in and the boat was heaved into place just before it went right past the landing stage. William and Mary, in something of a flurry, were able to alight and so the masque could proceed. However, all the music was pre-recorded, and because of the mooring hiccup the action was out step with the music. You know what it's like if you're watching something on film or television when the lips aren't synchronised with the words, it drives one round the bend. Well, so it was with several items of the masque performance. It was not until the scene where my dance happened that everything got back into sync Because I was able to get to my team and say to them, "When you go on to perform, start the dance from wherever the music has got to, not necessarily the beginning of what we have learned and rehearsed."

I had some good dancers, experienced enough to cope with that and the rest of the company followed suit.

I'm pleased to say, from there on in things went smoothly.

There was another little quirk that might amuse you. At the end of each evening, as an epilogue, Bess of Hardwick appeared in a spotlight on the flat roof of Chatsworth House and declaimed across the park, a request that the Dukes of Devonshire and their families would, in perpetuity, continue to be loyal in their support of England and their service to the people of Derbyshire. The actress playing Bess of Hardwick was pregnant and, by the time it got to the show, very pregnant. Both she and the Wardrobe mistress were totally unfazed by this, as they had an excellent solution to the appropriate visual image, which I share with you just in case it's ever useful. It was this: since Bess of Hardwick was in Elizabethan costume, providing the ruff that she wore around her neck was bigger in diameter than the size of the baby bump, no one would ever notice!

Devonshire 300 was a joyous success; the audiences were splendid, the duke was happy and, I reiterate, it didn't rain. However, on the last night you could divide the audience into two parts; the part that represented the great and good of Derbyshire and the part that were there representing corporate interests. The first group were all sporting oiled coats, woollen scarves and sensible shoes, comfortably warm. The other group had come in Gucci suits, pashminas casually tossed round shoulders and elegant footwear, stylish no doubt, but quietly freezing.

The very last part of the masque was spectacular: in a spotlight, a giant arm rose up from the waters of the lake and a voice declared across the parkland, in response to Bess of Hardwick, the promise that the Devonshires would serve the Crown and Derbyshire in the future, as they had in the past.

When the final performance was all over, I walked back to the dressing room marquee with 'my duke' and a couple of the other actor dukes.

One of them said to my duke "Was Sindon doing the voice at the end?"

My duke replied, "Yes, he was," and then the first duke said, "Was he pissed? He sounded pissed," and my Duke said, "Yes, he was."

Thus ended my week at Chatsworth sharing with the nobility a celebration of three hundred years of the dukedom. Bye-bye.

4. Another Tribute — Jubilee (Part1)

Hello everyone. The title of my tale today is, "The day that the Queen came." It could equally be called, 'The day that the rain came." When the Queen was celebrating her Golden Jubilee, as part of her 2002 National Tour, she came to visit Derby. I was part of the team that organised and mounted the celebration event which was held in 'Pride Park', the Derby County Football Club stadium. After the event was over, many of my friends asked me, "Did you meet the Queen?" the answer was, "No, thank goodness!"

Why, 'thank goodness'? Of course, I would have liked to meet the Queen, until that was, I saw myself in the outfit that I was provided with to wear as one of the official organisers! The next time you watch a big event, whenever that might be, just spare a thought for the staff who are required to wear a uniform designed by person or persons unknown, or a committee, or an alien. When I saw myself in the outfit that I was to wear I thought it was fairly... 'amazing'... useful word, as it can be interpreted as either negative or positive. I'll describe it to you: tight lycra trousers with stirrups under the feet — there might have been a time in my life when I looked good in such a garment but that was a very long time ago. On the top half, an outer garment of bright purple satin, very puffy, more puffy than my highest tog rated winter duvet, and actually made to fit someone several sizes bigger than myself; for my head, a baseball cap with a stiff brim and a little hole at the back for my ponytail to go through, if indeed I had a ponytail which I didn't; shades, dark glasses that wrapped right round the eyes to guard from the blaze of the sun, and then a little earpiece such as Madonna might wear so that all of the people on the organising team could be in contact with each other. I put the outfit on at home and went down to the back door, because my husband was working in the covered yard outside our back door and I wanted his opinion on me, in the said outfit. When I opened the back door, I discovered that he was 'potting out', a task that appears to involve many little polystyrene pots, a lot of gravel, a lot of peat, some pebbles and tiny plants all looking as though they'd lost the will to live days ago. All of this kit was arrayed on the rather rickety picnic table that we have in the covered yard. As I opened the door I said, "Well, what do you think?"

Whereupon my husband after a slight pause started to chuckle, then he started to laugh, then he started to cry and then he fell against the table and the pots and the peat and the stones and the pebbles and the plants went absolutely everywhere. I said, mustering all the dignity I could, "I take it you're not very impressed." And walked away leaving him to clear up the mess. The garment that he didn't see is the only part of the uniform that I still own, a tee shirt, a fairly straight forward tee shirt, purple in colour and on the back of it, appliquéd in pink satin, it says, 'JEAN 4'. The Queen was only introduced to those officials designated 1, 2 and 3. Quite apart from anything else, when I had the whole outfit on, I felt like one of the deep-sea divers of yesteryear that used to wear big heavy boots and a brass helmet and, on dry land, had difficulty in moving around.

I arrived at Pride Park at half past seven in the morning and it was raining. I left Pride Park at about half past seven in the evening and it was still raining. On that occasion, I was rather glad that I was a woman, because I went to the lavatory a couple of times and ladies, when they go to the lavatory, tend to sit down and that was the only relief that my feet had for the whole of that long and eventful day. Now very, very recently someone gave me an official programme of the event. They had been there in the audience, an audience of thousands, and I was pleased and surprised to discover that I had an official title. I was down in the programme as Stage Manager. What my job really was, was to make sure that the right people were performing in the arena, i.e., the football pitch of Pride Park, at the right moment of the day and I had copious lists of instructions to help make that work. In the morning the rehearsal, though wet, was fairly calm apart from the fact that there were constant interruptions. The police arrived, the firemen arrived, and the police helicopter flew overhead. There were sniffer dogs and there were security officials of all sizes, shapes and races, all endeavouring to make sure that everyone was safe, especially of course, the royal visitor. In actual fact, the people who were the least safe were the people who were going to perform any activity that involved running or jumping or dancing on the pitch arena, because the hallowed turf of Pride Park had been covered with very heavy-duty white plastic sheeting and that was sopping wet. It had, all day, a permanent film of water running over the top of it. How the gymnasts and acrobats were able to carry on, I really do not know, but they did.

In the morning, our little earpieces worked, and we were able to talk to each other. We were able to alert each other as to little problems that we could see, or something that wasn't going to work, or something that was going to not fit the timing allowed for it. Yes, the morning went quite calmly but then the real event was upon us. The crowds arrived in droves; entertainment had been set up outside the arena to keep the crowd happy while they were arriving and being shown in. For security reasons, only one entrance was open for the audience to come in. No one wanted to stay outside, because yes, you guessed, it was raining. Eventually, all were safety gathered in and under cover in the stands. The din inside the arena was tremendous, lots of people, tannoy systems blaring, recorded music playing, the rain pounding on the roof of the stands… and our little earpieces were not up to the job. For the whole of the afternoon, one could tell when one was being contacted, because one's earpiece hissed frantically, but sadly, one could not tell what was actually being said!

The moment had come! At any moment the Queen would arrive. She was going to be driven in, in a splendid limousine, deposited next to the VIP stand, welcomed by the Lord Lieutenant and go to her seat and then… Ah! But what then? What was going to happen to the car? The car couldn't drive out by circling the arena, unless I was able to warn all of the young people involved in the first item of the event that the car was going to come past before they could run onto the pitch. One of the things that my sheet of instructions did not say was what was going to happen to the car after the Queen got out. Near me, standing on one of the stands was a smart gentleman, tall, of military bearing, in a pinstriped suit, with a tiny little enamel badge in his lapel. I've been to Palace garden parties, and I knew that he was likely to be one of the Queen's security contingent, so I went up to him and I said, "Excuse me, but are you one of the Queen's security team?"

He replied, "Oh! My dear, I'm meant to be incognito."

I said, "Well fair enough, but *are* you one of the Queen's security contingent?"

He answered, "Oh! My dear, not to put too fine a point upon it, I am."

So, I said, "And what is going to happen to the car when the Queen has got out of it?"

He looked very crestfallen and said, "Oh! My dear, not to put too fine a point upon it, I haven't the faintest idea."

I then said, "I will go and discuss the matter with the driver once the Queen is out of the car."

And indeed, that's what I did. The Queen got out on one side of the car, and I went up to the driver on the other side, who rolled down his window and I asked him what he was going to do with the car, and he said, "Oh Gawd gal, I dunno".

Now, I am the granddaughter of a Cockney, I can cope with being called 'gal' and I said, "Presumably this car will go backwards."

Since most of the rear half was made of Perspex, there wasn't any problem with vision and the driver said, "Well. Yeah, suppose it might."

I said, "Then I suggest that I go and tell the performers waiting at the gate behind you, that they are not to stand in the way, as you will need to reverse out, and that, until you are safely clear, they are not to come into the Pride Park arena."

"Right!" he said, "Sounds like a plan, Duck." This is probably the greatest power I have ever wielded, and I am pleased to say that it worked. The car reversed out and only when I said that all was clear, were the young people waiting outside the gate allowed to enter and make the 'magic' happen. The 'magic' which I will share with you in just a moment.

5. Another Tribute — Jubilee (Part 2)

The chauffeur of the Queen's limousine was as good as his word and reversed out of the arena through the gateway by which he had arrived. I was glad to be wearing my much-deplored outfit, it meant the chauffeur had no fears that I was any sort of terrorist. No terrorist would be seen wearing an outfit like that! The reason I couldn't let the car drive round the perimeter road was because I knew that, dotted around the perimeter of the arena at strategic intervals, there were teams of young people with huge nets, which they were going to pull into the centre of the Pride Park pitch and the cue for doing that was when the Queen had been greeted and took her seat. Sadly, with our little earpieces not being reliable, I couldn't know that the children's chaperones would hear anything but frantic fizzing if I tried to send a warning message that a car was going to drive past.

When the Queen took her seat, the arena was suddenly filled with young people and monstrous nets. In each net there were hundreds of golden balloons, helium balloons, one balloon for each day of the Queen's reign, 365 x 50; that's a lot of balloons. The young person in charge of each team had a release mechanism and, when that was pulled, the nets opened, and the balloons floated free. Now, each balloon was on a string about eighteen inches long and at the bottom of the string was an identification tag. The idea was that the balloons, when released, would fly out over Derby and would eventually deflate and land. If anyone picked up a tag and returned it to the organisers they might be in luck, as the person finding the tag from the balloon that went the furthest would get a significant prize.

The nets of inflated balloons, however, couldn't be stored outside without getting sopping wet and there was nowhere big enough to store them inside. We're talking about nets of a huge volume. All of the balloons that had been on the outer edges of the nets had tags that were absolutely saturated. All of the balloons that were safely in the middle of the nets had totally dry tags and all of the balloons that had been neither in the middle nor on the outer edge, had damp tags. The wetter the tag the heavier the tag, so what happened? When the balloons were released from their nets, some of them soared up and away; some of them floated upwards and then just hovered; some of them stayed on the ground, not quite on the ground, but just as far off the ground as the length of string that they were attached to. The effect was amazing because the ones that flew free looked splendid as they took flight into the sky. The ones on the ground looked like flowers all over the white pitch, but most of the balloons were neither up nor down and made a golden ceiling that covered the pitch at the height of the roof of the covered stands. It was as splendid as it was surprising. I was told on good authority, the Lord Lieutenant, that the Queen was very impressed. She had smiled and said, "That must have taken a lot of work."

Of course, she knew what she meant; the moment was quite magical. The whole afternoon was quite stunning and the first things to get stunned were all the balloons on the ground, because someone had the forethought to equip each of the youngsters with a pin so that, before they left the arena, they could prick the balloons that were on the ground, otherwise they would have stayed there like flowers for the whole of the rest of the afternoon.

One or two of the events didn't actually happen. The County Wind Band did not play because getting expensive woodwind instruments sopping wet is not a good idea. On the other hand, some Asian drummers, who had been going to play to keep the audience entertained before they entered Pride Park were summoned, because they were all still there in the stands watching the proceedings and easy to find because of their colourful costumes. They played absolutely magnificently in the slot in the programme where the wind band would have been performing. When I said that I hoped that their instruments were not damaged by the rain, the leader of the team smiled at me and said,

"They're made of cow hide; the cows will have got wet lots of times."

A very philosophical attitude.

One group, that will stay in my mind forever, was a team of men who were going to do an act like the Keystone Cops, comic policemen.

When the right piece of music started for their item, I said, "Right, you're on now."

The leader said, "Do you mean us?" and I said, "Yes," and he said, "You mean in the middle of the arena?" and I said, "Yes," and he said, "When's that then?" and I said, "Now! Go now!"

Finally, he got the message. "Oh right! Come on lads, we're on now."

That exchange took place at the rehearsal in the morning. When they came off, he said to me, "Well, that was good fun, but we'll be in costume this afternoon, so you won't recognise us."

I replied that I was pretty sure I would. When it came to their moment in the afternoon performance, I said, "Right you're on now," and he said, "Do you mean us?" and I said, "Yes you!" and he said, "And when are we going on?" and I said, "You're going now. Now!"

When they were performing, they were very funny, very funny indeed. I looked on my list to see who the men in the group were. I found out that they really were policemen; in fact, the official title of the group was the Derbyshire Rapid Response Unit.

I had another note on my programme which was headed 'Dogs'. It said something like; sheep dogs at 3.25pm, police dogs at 3.27, dogs for the blind at 3.30, carer dogs at 3.33.

The dogs were impressive, they all did exactly what they were meant to do, at the time that they were meant to do it. I did get one urgent message handed to me on a soggy bit of paper and it asked me to sort out 'heavy equipment'.

What? How was I, albeit I had two helpers, going to sort out heavy equipment? And what heavy equipment? I was stumped, until a very under-clad young man, black, with Rastafarian dreadlocks approached me. He was in constant movement and said, "Whoa bro!" I thought that meant, hello, and I asked, "Are you one of the acrobatic team?"

He replied, "Oh Yea! Darlin' I am."

I said, "I gather that you use heavy equipment," and he said, "Oh Darlin', I *am* Heavy Equipment."

I had no comments to make to that, but it did explain to me in what way I had to sort out 'Heavy Equipment'. I had to prompt him and his fellow acrobats that it was now their moment of glory. 'Heavy Equipment' was the group's name, and they were magnificent, and brave, because leaping over huge gym boxes and doing vaults and somersaults and landing on gym mats that were covered in running water, I do not know how they didn't injure themselves.

When we got through to the end of the event, one of the people who stood out because of her use of the sound equipment was the Queen. She spoke slowly, and clearly, and everyone could understand every word. Many of the people who used the microphones that day produced lots of volume and boom but no articulation that was intelligible over the pounding of the rain on the roof of the covered stands and the noise of all of the people filling them. At the end of the proceedings, as the royal party were leaving the stadium, they walked down a line of the performers. One of the performers, a member of the company that my husband and I run, was dressed in the costume she had worn in the musical *Kismet*. It was diaphanous when dry, but when wet, very clinging and practically invisible to the eye. The Duke of Edinburgh peered at her and said, "It looks rather wet down there."

Was he really looking at her décolletage? Well, he might have been. The next night the young lady, so singled out, was at a scheduled rehearsal of our musical group and during the tea break my husband presented her with a spoof certificate that he had designed, printed and framed. It was a royal warrant: 'Purveyor of Titillation to the Titled'. The last time I visited her house it was hanging, as it has done for many years, in the downstairs lavatory. The day that the Queen came was a wonderful occasion with Her Majesty looking happy throughout and the performers determined that no rain was going to, in any way, put a damper on a celebration of which we were all proud. It's been fun remembering that day and sharing it with you. Thank you. Bye-bye.

Long-lived Ladies

My talk today is called "Long-lived Ladies: my mum, my nan, my grandma, my nana and my aunty." Gerald Durrell wrote a very famous book called *My Family and Other Animals* and I suppose, in a way, I'm emulating that book, but I'm only homing in on the female of the species. Long-lived ladies because all of those ladies made it into their 'nineties or beyond. On one occasion, I was being introduced and the president or chairman of the group said the talk was, "Long Live Ladies!" Well, I agree with that as well, so it doesn't matter which the title is.

First of all, let me introduce you to the ladies. I'm going to use the little word pictures that I wrote for that first occasion.

My mum — a force to be reckoned with, a people-person, unpredictable, with no sense of direction, but usually on the right track, a born raconteur.

My nan — a larger-than-life, snuff-sniffing, indomitable Cockney, who used to swear a lot, but insisted that she learned the swear words from a parrot that had been in the Navy.

My grandma — grand, a pillar of the parish, always well turned out, always well-informed, never without a hat, a hatpin or an opinion.

My nana — my great-grandmother, a powder-puff pink lady with a rod of iron as a backbone, charming and formal, maintaining a style against the odds.

My Aunty Kath — a pretty, sunny, caring woman with wavy shiny hair, twinsets, pearls, silk scarves; a television, a telephone and a telephone voice.

1. Introducing My Mum

When I was a child, my father only ever smacked me twice. The first occasion was an instinctive reaction to the fact that I had just hit him over the head with a cricket bat! I was about seven. It was my birthday. We'd had a birthday tea and one of my presents had been the said cricket bat. Behind our house there was a field, so after the meal, we had all trooped into the field for a game of cricket. Because it was my birthday and my bat, I was the first in. Now I've never been able to hit anything in a preconceived direction; in fact, very rarely have I ever managed to hit anything at all that I was meant to. On this occasion, I missed the ball completely and I was bowled out first ball, which my father, as umpire, loudly declared. There was only one bat, so he came to collect it from me, to give to the next person, who was going to be in. I had very definite other ideas. Instead of giving the cricket bat to him I whacked him with it, and he smacked me in an automatic response.

The second time he smacked me was when I was very rude about my mother — ruder than, at the time, I appreciated. How was that? Well, my mother was adopted. She was adopted when she was about two. My grandparents had always wanted children and although they had conceived children, they'd never managed to have a child that was healthy and lived, so they responded very promptly, when they saw an advertisement in the local paper saying, "*Small girl needs good home.*" As I understand it, when they went to the address given, there was a small girl being looked after by a very elderly woman, too old to be her mother. The lady's surname was Sage and that was about it — she either couldn't or wouldn't provide any other details. My grandparents gathered up my mum and that was that. These days, an adoption wouldn't be allowed to be as informal as that, but at that time, it was. My mum and her adoptive parents were an instant success with each other and two years later, my adoptive grandparents had a small boy they called Ernest, my uncle Ern, of whom I was very fond. My mum and Ern were good mates throughout all of their long lives. So, why was I rude about my mum and why did my dad smack me? Like most girls, I sometimes got a bit uppity and one day, when I was cheeky to my mum, she said, "Who do you think you're speaking to?" and I replied, "Well, we don't really know do we?" I don't think that, at whatever age I was then, I appreciated how rude I had been. I certainly hope not.

So, what can I tell you about my mum? My memories of my mum are great; we very rarely fell out with each other and when we did, we were both extremely articulate at arguing. My mum had no sense of direction. That is true. It's very difficult to have no sense of direction, because usually, if you have to make a decision about which way you're going to go, left or right, you've got a 50/50 chance of being right and she was always wrong, which suggests that her sense of direction was not only not very good, it was perverse. But there were a great many things that she *was* good at. Another one she wasn't good at, was sewing. She did once make a very pretty little dress for one of my dolls. It looked splendid, until I tried to put it on the doll and that didn't work, because she had forgotten to leave any holes in the ends of the sleeves for the doll's arms to go through. I also remember an occasion when my brother, a boy of about twelve or thirteen, was found, one morning, by me, when I got up early, sitting on the chair in the kitchen, sewing, or trying to sew, his jodhpurs. The top half of him was very smartly attired, because he was about to perform in a gymkhana and the lower half, just long, skinny, spindly boy, teenage legs.

All he said to me, giving me a glance of despair, was, "You would think she could sew!"

Well, she couldn't, but the positive outcome of that was that my brother and I have always been able to sew very well.

My mother was also wonderful at the 'bon mot' and I'll tell you about one of them. I was a young adult, and we were, as a family in the car, driving on the Isle of

Grain. There is a large oil refinery on the Isle of Grain and as we were nearing the gatehouse, where there was a security guard, my mother said, "Stanley, slow down a bit as we go past the gates."

Stanley, my dad, dutifully slowed down and didn't ask why. When we got near the gates, my mother rolled down the window on her side, leant out and said, in her best voice, "Young man, do you know your chimney's on fire?"

The young man managed to maintain a perfectly calm face and simply replied, "Yes madam."

When we got to the end of our journey and I got out of the car, I quietly said to my dad, "Dad, did Mum not know that's the way they burn off surplus gas, or was she joking?"

My dad said, "Well darling, I've only been married to her for about thirty years, so I'm not sure yet."

I'll tell you some more another time.

2. My Mum (Part 2)

Continuing my stories about my mother, I'm going to concentrate today on some of her excursions into interior decorating, but first, I need to remind anyone that's listening, that all the stories I tell you are true, because some of them sound as though I extricated them from a sitcom. Before I start with the interior decorating excerpts, I must just round off my chat yesterday about my mother and needlework.

This one particularly features my father. My father was a good-looking, charming, quiet, well-spoken gentleman and very rarely did he get roused, but when he did, he could always make his point felt, usually without raising his voice. Imagine this, it is teatime in our kitchen. There at the kitchen table my brother, my mother and I are sitting ready to start our evening meal. The back door opens and in walks my father, home from work. He gives us a cursory nod of greeting but doesn't say anything. He goes to the cupboard in the kitchen and takes out from the floor of the cupboard a cobbler's last. If you know what one of those is, fair enough, if you don't, it's a metal object, like a shoe tree, with three metal feet of different sizes, each of which is designed to face in a different direction. Cobblers put boots and shoes on them when they're resoling them. My father also takes from the cupboard, from his toolbox, a mallet. He comes to the table, takes off one shoe and one sock and still doesn't say a word. So, there's my mother saying, "What's the matter Stanley? Stanley what are you up to?"

Me saying, "What are you doing, Dad?" and my brother saying, "What's that, Daddy?"

My father didn't answer at all. When he had taken his sock off, he solemnly put it onto the biggest of the feet on the shoe tree, picked up the mallet and solemnly hammered his sock. Having done that, he removed the sock from the shoe tree, put the shoe tree and the mallet back into the cupboard, sat down at his place at the table and solemnly passed to my mother, the sock. Only then did he say, "That was a formal protest, brought about by the pain I have endured all day, as a result of your darning. Darling!" My mother's darning. My father's sock had a hole in it, a hole about two inches (5cm) in diameter and my mother had mended the hole in my dad's sock by doing a running thread stitch, round the circumference of the hole, and then pulling the whole thing tight and fastening off the thread. My father had spent all day walking on a nasty knot of screwed-up fabric that was now the middle of what had been the hole. My mother looked aghast but didn't lose her temper. She instantly came up with a solution. She turned to me and said, "Jean, you can darn."

She turned to my father and said, "In future, give your 'holey' socks to your daughter."

Now, interior decorating: my mother was very house proud, and our house always looked clean, nice and smart. My mother would always be sweeping or dusting some trace of dirt or debris which only she could see. My father referred to all of her cleaning implements as her toys and I believed him. I'm sorry to say, that one Christmas, I bought my mother a new dustpan and brush for her Christmas present and, what's even worse, she thanked me for it. She also liked moving the furniture around, so living in our house was quite exciting, because you never quite knew, from one day to the next, where anything would be positioned in the room, which meant a bit of a circular tour sometimes if you were looking for something. She unfortunately caught a disease, which at that time was prevalent, it was called, 'Fablon fever'. I don't know if you know what Fablon was. I don't know if you can still get it. You used to be able to buy it in Woolworths. Fablon was rolls of self-adhesive paper which had patterns on them. You could cut it, and you could stick it onto a surface if you wanted to decorate the surface, or make the surface have a shiny top, or a matte top. I still have some where the non-sticky side looks like green baize, and that's been quite useful over many years, if ever I've occasionally, wanted to line a drawer or something like that. My mother bought a roll of red mottled Fablon because one of the surfaces in the kitchen was a bit, sort of, scuffed and she put the Fablon on and liked the result. She had, of course, some Fablon left; she hadn't used the whole roll, so she decided to embark on covering another aspect of the kitchen surface top. Yes! You can guess! She ran out of Fablon. So, she had to buy another roll and so it went on. It only stopped when even she, herself, decided that our kitchen was really rather overdone with mottled red and that the Fablon era must end.

She was also very good at getting out the toolbox, if a job, that she'd asked my dad to do (he was very good at household jobs) had not been done quickly enough for her. Our kitchen table wobbled somewhat, and she decided, one day, that she would just sort this out. So somehow, when she was in on her own, she managed to tip the table up on its side, get my father's hacksaw and chop a bit off one of the legs. When the table was put back onto its legs, it wobbled rather more than it had done to start with. So, never-say-die, she did the same thing again, with a different leg, and so on, and so forth. That game ended when, my father, finding the result, the table still wobbly and now rather low, said, if she carried on any more, he would remove the table from the kitchen and put it in front of the sofa in the sitting room because it was now more the height of a coffee table. That was exaggerating and the wobble was dealt with, as it always had been, before she embarked on the chopping off of legs, by folding a piece of paper and sticking it under the shortest leg.

The pièce de resistance of my mother's interior decorating at that time, was to do with a wallpaper bale. My parents decided that they wanted to wallpaper the sitting room and they wanted a flamboyant wallpaper as they were weary of magnolia. They went to the DIY shop, and they bought an end of line 'bargain bundle'. The paper in question was a deep wine colour with rather spectacular silver palm trees on it. My dad had done a calculation to make sure there were enough rolls of paper in the bale to cover the walls of the room, but he had failed somewhat, when taking into account the 'repeat' of the said pattern. Now, one of the alcoves near the fireplace in our sitting room had a pipe that ran right across the middle of it — always a bit of an eyesore, even when painted magnolia. One day my father, brother and I came home from work/school and, lo and behold, the paper was up on the wall in the alcove and the pipe had been boxed in with wood to make a shelf. Under the pipe the wallpaper was upside down; above the pipe the wallpaper was the right way up. The new shelf had been painted in pale green, rather surprisingly, because all the rest of the paint work in the room was white. We congratulated my mother on putting up the shelf and finishing the papering. Eventually, my brother was bold enough to ask why the palm trees under the new shelf were upside down. My mother explained that this was the only way the last bit of wall could be covered with the last piece of wallpaper, if the trunks of the palm trees were to line up. After a pause, to take this in, I asked, "Why is the shelf pale green?"

"It's not pale green," said my mother, "It's Eau de Nile."

I must have still looked blank, so she continued, "Don't you get it? The shelf is the river Nile, the palm trees above the shelf are on the bank of the Nile and the palm trees below are their reflections in the water."

There was no answer to that. I'll tell you some more another time.

3. My Nan and my Grandma

When I was a small child, my grandfather made for me, a little attaché case. it was wooden, had a nice little handle, a lock and, what I assumed was my name, stencilled on the top. I was very proud of it, and I kept all my treasures in it. One day when I was telling my grandad how pleased I was with my little case I happened to say, "Grandad, you have put J-E-A-H on the top and you should spell Jean, J-E-A-N."

My grandfather explained to me carefully, that he hadn't put my name on the lid at all; the letters, J. E. A. H. were my initials: Jean, Evelyn, Amy, Hawkins. I had never realised that.

I was Jean, because I wasn't John! My nan, sure before I was born, that the child, me, would be a boy, had knitted baby garments and had embroidered them with J for John, because John Hawkins was a knight. In the event, I was a girl, so I was Jean, which Nan was glad about, because, by then, she had found out that John Hawkins was also a pirate. The E was Evelyn, my mum. She liked being Evelyn; she didn't mind being Eve; she couldn't bear it if anyone called her Eva. The A was for my nan, Amy. It was the name that I liked least as a young girl; now, it's probably the name that, of my three names, is the most popular. I tell you all this, because I'm moving on from talking about my mother, to talk about her mother, always referred to by me as Nan, and my father's mother always known as Grandma.

The two ladies were physically quite alike — big women, but they were, in every other respect, very, very different. My mother's mother was a Cockney through and through. She really did sniff snuff, and she really did have a parrot, which, she insisted, was the one who had taught her lots of swear words, because the parrot had been in the Navy. My recollection of her, is that she always sat 'in state 'in the same chair in the corner of the living room and she wore, over her clothes, an all-engulfing floral overall, the sort where you put both arms in and the front, sort of overlaps, with a tie belt that goes through a slot and round the back and then ties at the front. Have you got that? It seemed to me that she always wore an overall and that every year, at Christmas, she had a present of three new ones. I don't know who bought them for her, it's possible she bought them for herself; one on, one in the wash and one spare. The only occasions when I ever remember her, still sitting in that chair, but without the overall, was on one significant birthday, one significant wedding anniversary and Christmas afternoon — not in the morning, you understand, because she always cooked the Christmas lunch. She was an excellent cook; she could always make a meal that tasted splendid, quite something, when you consider that she cooked all the way through the wartime and the long years of rationing that followed.

Her cooking became, in a way, my cooking. I would watch her cook or help her cook and I can remember saying one day, when she was showing me how to make bread pudding, not summer pudding, bread pudding that's like a cake, "Do you put an egg in it, Nan?" and she would say, "No dear, unless you've got one."

Then I would say, "Does it have currants, Nan?" and she would say, "If you can spare some."

She had, I suspect, the cleanest kitchen floor in Christendom. Why? Because in her quite large kitchen there was a big built-in boiler and every Monday all the washing would get piled into this boiler and boiled, literally, and when it boiled, it inevitably boiled over. For many years I would go to my nan's house for lunch from school and I can remember every Monday coming in the back door and having to tread very carefully over the sudsy water that always covered the kitchen floor. That meant that, on Monday, we always had cold meat, for lunch. In fact, since Nan was a creature of habit, you could tell which day of the week it was by what the menu was, or vice-versa.

Every Christmas we would have rabbit. People don't eat rabbit very much these days, but my recollections of rabbits are fond and festive. All through the year, there would be a rabbit in a hutch in my nan's garden and I would feed, stroke and pet the rabbit. I don't think I was very bright in some respects, because it never seemed to occur to me that, after Christmas, the rabbit was always different to the one that had been there before Christmas. That is, until one year, just before the holiday, I opened the door of the walk-in larder and there, hooked on the back of the door, with wooden staves holding it open, was the rabbit that I had been feeding and petting all year. It was being 'hung', that's a term for dealing with things like game. I had another clue as well, that year when we opened our presents. My present was a beautiful pair of fur mittens. I think I wept little, when I realised that for years, the rabbit I had been eating at Christmas was the rabbit I had been petting all year. But when Christmas day came, which was a few days later, I still tucked in to my Christmas meal.

My nan was always full of stories, especially stories about when she was a girl in service. She told me one about the early morning bells: the bell to wake up, the bell to be ready for your breakfast and, before those, the bell to be ready for the bells.

"What can that mean?" I hear you ask. Well, Nan lived and worked in a great big house and one of the things in big houses was that, sometimes, there would be lots of guests, so the first bell was to warn any guests that had 'strayed', to get back into their own beds before the servants brought breakfast trays.

My other grandmother was quite different, a pillar of society. She taught the piano and lived in Rochester. If you looked at a map, you might have some doubt as to whether she lived in Rochester or Chatham. I think she lived on the line between the two, but because my grandmother had some illusions of grandeur, she, of course, as I previously explained, lived in Rochester! I think that my mum was a little bit wary of this grandmother, who I always called Grandma, who would arrive at our house like a galleon in full sail. She would remove her hat and the hat pin with a flourish. For some years, I was sure that when she put the hat and the pin back on, the pin went right through her head. One of my favourite memories of her, was the day that my brother had been out catching tadpoles. On the windowsill of the lavatory, which wasn't quite 'down the garden path', but opposite the back door, he had put a jar with some pretty grimy pond water and lots of tadpoles. Grandma came to visit and needed to use the facilities. After a little while there were dreadful cries of distress and noises off. My brother, my mother and I rushed to see what the problem was. The door of the lavatory was open, there was smashed glass on the floor, greenish, brackish water all over the place and innumerable tadpoles wriggling around on various bits of the windowsill, the floor, and my grandmother's ample bosom. My mother flapped around, a bit ineffectually, trying to get the water and the tadpoles off my grandma. I decided that I ought to try to look as if I was being useful, though in truth, I didn't know what to do and my brother sort of retreated. Taking control, my grandma said firmly, "Eve, stop messing around! Rescue these creatures! My clothes will wash! I will wash! Do you not realise that tadpoles are a protected species?"

We had underestimated a woman who was never to be underestimated.

She was very good at making nice cakes and cooked on a well-used, well loved, gas stove. At that time, North Sea gas was the new thing, and everyone had to have their gas cookers modified for the new source of gas. The Gas Board published that they would do this modification free of charge, for anyone who had a gas stove in working order. Two unsuspecting young engineers came to my grandma's house, and she gave them tea and home-made cakes, which they appreciated. She then took them to show them the gas stove that needed to be modified. The two young men blanched somewhat, because the gas stove was home-made, made by my grandfather. Few people have a home-made gas stove.

When the young men said, "Oh, we can't do anything about that!" she got the advertisement from the paper, which was to hand, poised and ready, and showed it to them. Pointing to the plate of cakes that they had just sampled, she asked, "Was the gas stove in working order?" They had to admit that it was. "Therefore," she went on, "I must be entitled to a new cooker, if you will not modify this one."

She got her new gas stove! What my two grandmothers had in common was that they were both indomitable.

4. My Nana and my Aunty Kath

Today, I'm going to tell you about my great-grandmother. I always referred to her as Nana, Nana Hawkins. For the last four years of her life, she lived in our house. That wasn't easy, because it was only a three-bedroom house and, in order to accommodate her, she was given the biggest bedroom. I had the smallest bedroom and my parents had to move into the middle bedroom, with my younger brother's bed in a curtained-off corner of the same room. We made all of these modifications in order to give a charming old lady a nice home. Besides her room, which was quite a good size, Nana had a sort of walk-in wardrobe, at least that's what it was intended to be, but my father had put in there, for her use, a gas ring, a commode, a washstand with a jug and basin and some shelf space. She never, ever, referred to her "room" she always referred to her "set". The only time I've ever heard the use of the word "set" to mean a suite of rooms was when young men about town used to talk about having a "set" at the Albany.

She did not choose to become part of the family in the sense that you might expect. Nana was a small lady, always immaculately groomed, with a slight air of Maggie Smith about her. Her room was her kingdom; whenever you went into it, it always looked beautiful and never showed any signs of the fact that it was a bedroom. Some sort of transformation, which I never witnessed, occurred every night before she went to bed, and by the time she was up and about in the daytime, a second transformation had put her room back to being a sitting room or drawing room. I remember a nice, embroidered quilt on what at night was the bed, which by day was tucked into an alcove, with a pile of cushions along the long side of it, so that it looked like a luxurious divan. Nana never entertained except by appointment, though if my brother and I wished to go to say "Hello!" to her, that was all right, providing we knocked at the door and waited until we were asked in. She would, from time to time, invite one or other, or both of us, to come and take tea with her. Sometimes she chose to eat with us, the family, but often my mother would take up Nana's main meals on a tray. I never appreciated at the time, but of course one doesn't when one's a child, how much work that involved for my mother.

The story that I have chosen to tell about Nana is, well, in retrospect, hilarious; it wasn't hilarious at the time. It was the only occasion, I recollect, that my mother and my nana had, what you might call, a falling out. It was brought about by the fact that, although Nana could boil a kettle and, perhaps even make a little toast in her room, she couldn't cook in her room. On this particular occasion, she had decided to make herself a little rice pudding. She had come to the house kitchen, my mother's kitchen, made the rice pudding and put it in the oven to cook. As it happened, my brother, who has always been a keen sportsman and, from a very young age, a great tennis player, was going to play in a tournament that day. When he was gathering together his whites, he discovered that the socks he wanted to wear were still somewhat damp from the last time they had been washed. My mother, knowing that the oven was on, and it was only on at a low heat, put my brother's damp socks, clean damp socks, straight from being washed, into a baking tray and put them in the bottom of the oven. When my nana came downstairs to see whether her little rice pudding was done, she opened the oven door, saw the socks, looked unutterably mortified, said not a word, stormed back to her set and quickly reappeared wearing her hat. This was because she never deemed it appropriate to go out without her hat. Where was she going? Well, not a very long journey, she was going from the stove in the kitchen to the dustbin in the garden. She retrieved her rice pudding from the oven, stormed out of the back door and with great ceremony threw the rice pudding, complete with dish, into the dustbin. She came back in, exuding bristling indignation from every pore — she didn't say a word and neither did my mother, — that would have been undignified.

That brings us to Aunty Kath. Aunty Kath was the wife of Uncle Ted. Uncle Ted was my father's elder brother. Kath was a charming, sunny lady, one who was a born conciliator and always made things go smoothly if she possibly could. She was vital to every party that our family ever had. Why? Because she had a talent that the rest of us didn't share, she could slice bread thinly, evenly and neatly, and in the days before you could buy sliced bread, to have someone around who could make neat slices for sandwiches and the like, was an invaluable asset. So, every time there was a family event, for example, a tea party, nothing could start until Aunty Kath arrived, armed with her own knife, which she had used so many times that the middle of the blade had a waist, where it had worn away. I used to watch, horror-stricken, as she used it, because I was sure that one day, it would snap. She would almost invariably, also bring with her a trifle. She made extremely good trifles, they tasted very nice. They always tasted much nicer than they looked, because she took pleasure in sprinkling multi-coloured sugar hundreds and thousands on the top of her trifles for decoration and she always sprinkled them on too soon, so that, by the time the trifle had been wrapped in a tea towel and taken in a basket to whatever event it was going to grace, the sugar colouring had all run, so whatever the design might have been, my aunty Kath's trifles always had a sort of splodgy, muddy, pinky-grey top to them. To this day, if I make trifles, or flans that need decoration on the top, I leave putting on the decoration to the very, very last minute before I serve them, because I do not want my dessert creations to suffer the same gloopy tops as Aunty Kath's otherwise delicious puddings.

Aunty Kath was beautifully spoken, also her house was very well-appointed. The house had a front room, a front room which was always cold and rather forbidding and, as I can recollect, only got used on very high days and holidays. It had within it, my Uncle Ted's organ, in the days before one had electronic organs and someone had to pump it, if he was going to play; often that someone was me. Ted was a church organist and choirmaster in his spare time. The house also had a television with a fourteen-inch screen, and they had the television in time for the Coronation. Their house also had a telephone and Aunty Kath had a telephone voice that would shame Hyacinth Bucket, or rather, 'Hyacinth Bouquet', if you can remember who she was. I honestly believed, that in order to have a telephone, you had to have a telephone voice. I used to enjoy going to their house. I watched *Quatermass* on their little television, hiding behind the sofa with my hands in front of my eyes, but with my fingers spread apart, so that when the nasty bits came, I could close my fingers together and hide down behind the sofa. Oh! It was so exciting to watch something that was scary.

Aunty Kath had phrases. She always used to say, if something was bad, that it was, "Something chronic". Not until I was a grown-up, did I learn that 'chronic ' meant something ongoing and long-lasting. I previously believed that it meant, 'imminent', 'immediate', 'acute 'or 'regretful'. Also, she was always trying to quieten the four of, 'We Kids'. Four, because there was me and my brother, my cousin Brenda, same age as me, and my cousin Diane, a little bit younger than Brenda, but a bit older than my brother. We were competitive, all of us, and so when we were together, although we weren't riotous in a physical sense, we could be very noisy and one of Aunty Kath's famous expressions was, "Why don't we all play a quiet game of Chinese Chequers?" As I recall, we rarely ever did. I enjoyed my childhood, but in telling you these tales it would appear to be something of a sitcom. It didn't feel like that at the time, but it did feel happy. I'll leave the last word to my mother.

It is true that my mother was not very good at directions, but she was very, very good, at people and friendships. She made friends wherever she went and had the enviable talent of always being able to remember people's names and what they had been up to the last time she saw them, even if the gap was a long while. I once had to ask her, when I wanted to make a speech about my past boyfriends, who they all were, because she had stayed friends with all of them. Now the story. At a tea party my mother, one day, produced a pair of Y-fronts and asked the assembled men: my father, my uncle, my brother, my husband and my son, if they belonged to any of them. They all insisted that they did not. Whereupon, my mother said, "Oh well, they must belong to that Dutchman I made friends with on a coach trip. There was silence, then laughter, and no explanation was ever offered. If she didn't offer one, why should I? Goodbye.

Call Me Madam

1. Titles and Key Staff

Hello, the title of my story today is "Call Me Madam". Now, there's a famous musical called *Call Me Madam*, by Irving Berlin and, some years ago, I had great fun playing the role of Madam in *Call Me Madam*. It's about a woman who was the first female American ambassador, loosely based on a true story. In the musical, the woman is very rich, full of vitality, lots of joie de vivre and absolutely no clue what she's doing. Fortunately, because her heart's in the right place, not only does she get to be the heroine of the plot, she gets a man as well. This *Call Me Madam* has nothing to do with the stage or musicals, except in a sense it is about performing. I taught for thirty-four years and for the first half of those years, I was referred to by my pupils either as, Miss Hawkins, Mrs Bishop or Mrs Gemmell or, most often, Miss. When I became head of a big school in Nottingham, my predecessor as head teacher, a man, had decreed that all the women on the staff would be referred to as Madam, so from that moment on I was Madam. It's better to be called Madam than Miss, if only 'for one reason, when children are peeved or upset or grumpy they go, 'Mi-i-i-i-iss'. You can't do that with a two-syllable word, it's very difficult to slur a two-syllable word, so, for sixteen or so years I was head of a big comprehensive school and "Call Me Madam" was the order of the day.

If you've ever been new to a big organisation and, especially if you're going to be the boss of the big organisation, there are people who you have to get to know and make sure they're on your side because without their support your life isn't going to work very well. One of the first people is your secretary. For years and years, I had at that school a splendid secretary, but she would talk to me sometimes in code. She would signal her feelings or her intentions in various non-verbal ways. She belonged to an association which was called The National Association of Administrators and Secretaries in Schools and Colleges. Not a name that trips easily off the tongue, the acronym for it was NAASSC. She had a badge that she wore, a very splendid affair that always used to remind me of the sort of Celtic brooch that holds a plaid on one's shoulder, if one is in Highland dress. All the letters of NAASSC were intertwined and when I first saw it, the only three letters that stood out on that badge were S.A.S. After I got to know her well, not to mention various other school secretaries that I met over the years, I realised that SAS was as good a title for the person wearing it as any other that I could think of.

Often, in my official capacity, I would have visitors to my office and my secretary looked after my diary. If it was a member of staff who came to see me about something, they would usually be offered some coffee in one of the almost washed-up mugs that all the rest of us used all of the time. A visitor of slightly higher rank would get one of those green cups and saucers with ridges around the cups that there must be millions of — they must have been used in every government office or building in the kingdom. A still higher-ranking guest would get the Crown Derby tea set but that meant I couldn't have more than six guests in that category because there were only six cups and saucers in the Crown Derby tea set. If my guest was the pinnacle of significance, there would be a plate with biscuits and the plate would have a doily! Now, in my office, my desk was under a fluorescent light and like most fluorescent lights it had a bit of a mind of its own. Sometimes it would be as good as gold and sometimes it would flicker and drive me round the bend, but I'm a physicist, so had no problem in dealing with my flickering fluorescent light. I would climb up onto my desk, take off my high-heeled shoe and give the fluorescent tube a fairly hefty whack, it usually worked. One day I was standing on my desk with only one shoe on, the other one in my hand, whacking my fluorescent light into submission, just as my secretary showed in a 'doily quality' visitor, a very smart gentleman in uniform with more braid than you would have thought humanly possible. I thought it was funny and laughed, he thought it was funny and laughed, but my secretary was absolutely mortified. I feel she thought I'd let the side down entirely and I don't think she spoke to me other than in the absolute line of duty for about a fortnight.

We were working in the school at the time when computers were starting to be the mode of operation in offices, but the Education Department hadn't decided to issue schools with them yet and it was still in the days when we school heads didn't control our own budgets. I could send in an order for a piece of equipment if it was under a certain price and I worked out that if I sent in three such requisitions I could buy a Canon technical typewriter, or at least the components of the typewriting facility of a computer, a screen and a keyboard and the hard disc. Canon duly sent me the three different bits which had to be assembled and to assemble them they sent Malcolm. Malcolm was young, Malcolm was charming, and my secretary, whose name was Dorothy, fell in love with Malcolm almost instantly. He stayed with us for a fortnight and thanks to him the transition from Dorothy, declared technophobe, to Dorothy master of something very close to a word processor, went painlessly. Whoever appointed that young man knew exactly what they were doing. I think Canon showed much forethought in loaning Malcolm to us, all positive apart from the fact that when he left, we did have to endure a few days of withdrawal symptoms.

Another person whom you have to become friendly with, more or less straight away, is the cook. Our cook was splendid, a pin-thin wiry soul, a woman who was indefatigable, she could muster chips for hundreds of hungry teenagers at the drop of a hat, tho' she could get pretty grumpy when put upon; when a year head forgot to tell her that the whole of year something, were going to be out all day, or that everybody in such and such a group was going off school in the morning and wouldn't be back by lunch break, etc. Every now and again she would go on the obligatory training course. I soon discovered that when she came back from a training course, one had to be very careful how complimentary one was about her new menu choices. I particularly remember an occasion when she came back from a course having been advised that serving moussaka was a good thing. Her moussaka was very good. I said so effusively, and that was a mistake, because it seemed that we had moussaka pretty well every day for weeks thereafter.

The day I want to share with you was Valentine's Day. Now, it was fairly usual at Christmas, when it was the school Christmas lunch, that there would be festive decorations in the canteen. The ladies behind the hatch would wear festive hats and tinsel and the meal would be festive, but we'd never done anything festive on

Valentine's Day. On this occasion the cook had been on a course, so, when we went into the lunchroom, there were posters, there were love hearts, there were 'Happy Valentine's Day' signs and special additions to the menu. You could tell it was Valentine's Day, because the iced buns were iced in pink, normally they were iced in white. The meringues — cook was very good at meringues — had little cream love hearts on them and it was all very pretty. I had been teaching a physics lesson to a group of senior boys and, as it was customary in the school that one ate with pupils, I went along the serving hatch with some of the young men that I'd been working with on either side of me. I stopped and congratulated the cook on her efforts for Valentine's Day and she said, "Yes, it is going quite well, but it's a shame I couldn't think of anything for the main course that signified Valentine's Day."

At which point I, unfortunately, said to her, "Well, what is the main course today?" and she solemnly replied, "Toad in the hole."

I think the boys on either side of me were in agony. They, of course, thought her answer was hilarious, but, since they were standing next to their head teacher, they were not sure whether laughing was appropriate, until they discovered, to their relief, that I was grinning broadly. The only person who didn't get the innuendo and didn't see what was so funny was the cook! Bye-bye!

2. Caretaker and 'The Works'

Hello! If you're going to work in any sort of big organisation, one of the people that you have to have on your side is the caretaker. The caretaker oils the wheels, literally. Now one way to keep a caretaker on your side is to be prepared to go and look at things, to drop everything, spring to your feet and go and look at something when he says, "Madam, you must come and look at this."

When you get there, you usually find you have not actually got to do anything except, make an appropriate comment, so a 'Comment Bank' is a good idea. The comments could be, 'Oh how splendid!', or 'Oh you can't imagine they would do that!' or, 'That must have taken you such a long time.' Woe betide you, if you give the wrong comment for the wrong event. My advice under those circumstances is, 'If you can't be truthful, be vague!'

Now my caretaker and I got on particularly good terms over the crisis of the Potato Puffs. I don't know if you can still buy Potato Puffs, but they came in bags like crisps. They were made of potato, like crisps, but they were a bit like balloons, filled with nothing but air, so the volume appeared to be considerable, and you could munch quite a lot of them without actually consuming any calorific content that was significant at all. The pupils at my school had a school council; they had it before I joined as head and I decided that, though it existed in name, it wasn't actually doing anything very much. So, one of the things that I instituted, with a fair few qualms on the part of some of the other members concerned, was to invite a pupil from the school council to part of each governor's meeting. That way the pupils could see that sometimes, when I asked for something, the answer was, usually for good reason, "No". Thus, they could understand that when they asked for something, the answer might also be, "No".

One of the things the pupils had agitated for was a tuck shop, as we didn't have one. I got a few of the senior pupils to agree that if I found a space for them to operate from, they would have a rota whereby they would look after such a shop — and so it was. The space that they operated from was not very big, a fairly large broom cupboard or walk-in larder, that sort of size, so all of the tuck items that they bought had to be reasonably small so that they could be stored in boxes in the tuck shop, i.e., the cupboard. When it was lunch, or break, the pupils in charge would set up a little table outside of the door of their emporium and sell the goodies. It worked quite well, especially when I discussed with the pupils that were running the shop the idea of having a list on the wall of the goods that sold well. Only when a box of whatever was popular was coming to an end would they order more as there wasn't room in the little store to have more than one box of anything. That seemed to be fine until one day the caretaker came to my office and said, "Madam, you must come and look at these Potato Puffs."

Well of all the things I'd looked at before — I'd looked at newly polished hall floors; I'd looked at repairs that the caretaker had done himself; I'd looked at the bit of the wall of the drama hut that was rotting... I had never looked at Potato Puffs. I got up from my desk and followed him. He took me, surprisingly, to a storage area under the school stage, it was long and thin, the same size as the school stage and bleak, but it was full of large cardboard boxes and each cardboard box was a box of Potato Puffs. I thought, *how can this possibly be?* The answer was simple, the caretaker, trying to be helpful, had, whenever the wholesale lorry came with Potato Puffs, taken the Potato Puffs and put them under the stage, always leaving just one box of Potato Puffs in the tuck shop room, which meant that my volunteer helpers every week re-ordered Potato Puffs because there was only one box left. Oh dear! What to do? Well, we had to have a system to cope with this glut of Potato Puffs. I'm pleased to say in those days people weren't terribly worried about sell-by dates and Potato Puffs didn't seem to deteriorate particularly.

When there's mostly nothing there, there's not very much that can go wrong. So, we had an embargo on everything that the tuck shop sold except Potato Puffs and sold them at a much-publicised reduced price, just the price that we had to pay for them. I am pleased to say that the stock went down quite quickly, and normal service was resumed. The caretaker, realising that his attempts to be helpful had in part generated the problem, didn't say a word and I didn't say a word either, but from then on, we were good friends and over the years got to know each other quite well.

Actually, he got to know me rather better than I got to know him, but I wasn't aware of that until the day that I left the school. When I retired from being a head teacher to became general secretary of a trade union, I had a party and, of course, at the party there was a cabaret. Various items of the cabaret were put on by the pupils and staff and, of course, were designed to poke a little bit of fun at me — mostly gentle fun, I'm pleased to say. I was happy to join in the laughter, until to my amazement the caretaker, a guest at the party, by then retired, but still living close to the school, was part of the cabaret. He proceeded to describe an occasion when he had seen rather more of me than I had ever intended. Now you have to know that my office had one window, which looked straight on to the drive leading up to the main door of the school, and one door into my office which came directly from the school entrance hall, but there was another glass-panelled door, which came into my office from the secretary's kingdom. Now, even in those days, I was very much involved in the theatre and one night, after school had ended, I had pulled down the venetian blind of the outside window, locked the door that was to the entrance hall and proceeded to take off my workday clothes and put on the evening dress that I was planning to wear at the concert, that I was going to sing in. I had no idea, for years, that the event was witnessed. When I had probably nothing much on at all above my waist, the caretaker, doing his rounds to lock up, had come into my office through the door from the secretary's domain. I hadn't heard him, and he had had the grace, when he saw me, rather a lot of me, to retire very quietly, but, as they say, the truth will out. As you can imagine, everybody loved that story.

The other thing I'm going to tell you about is the Works Department. In those days, schools didn't maintain their own budgets and if you wanted a job done, you had to send in a requisition of some sort. Our school Gym had changing rooms which opened to the outside world and there was a winding path from the changing rooms round onto the school field. There was also a shrubbery with rather prickly bushes that went alongside the school field. The short route from the gym to the field was straight across the shrubbery and over years and years, hundreds of intrepid teenagers had taken the shortcut regardless of the prickly shrubs and had generated a hard-baked earth path. In the summertime that was fine, because the ground was hard baked, but not so in the winter, when countless feet generated mud, and no amount of saying to the pupils, 'You must go round on the path' actually succeeded in getting them to go round on the path. I asked, and asked, and asked, the Works Department to put some tarmac down to make an official route of the shortcut from the gym to the field, but it didn't happen. I lost count of how many times I phoned, until one day the Works Department phoned me. My secretary picked up the phone and she said, "It's someone from the Works Department on the phone. Do you want to speak to him?"

I said, "Yes please!" and the voice on the phone said, "If you want that bit of tarmac, you can have it, even if we have to have a whip-round in the office to pay for it."

Well, I got my tarmac, but not the last laugh, because the tarmac provided was bright orange. When I phoned back to say thank you, not to complain about the colour, I didn't get through to the Works Department boss, but I did hear someone in the distance say, "If that's Jean Gemmell, tell her I'm out."

3. Crime and Punishment

Hello everybody. My talk this evening, which is part of "Call me Madam", could be subtitled "Crime and Punishment". Fortunately, in all my years at the secondary school where I was boss, we didn't actually have that much crime, but the first time I needed police intervention was when I'd only been there for about a fortnight. The situation was, that some of the boys from my school got into an altercation on our school field with some of the boys from another school that was having a Teachers' Training Day holiday. Because sorting out the melée was going to involve young people that were not our pupils, I thought we had better have some police presence, so I phoned the local police station. At that time, though I knew that the police station was very near, I didn't know that it was just a bungalow, in a street of bungalows, only distinguishable from its neighbours by having a slightly wider drive, so that several vehicles could park there. The receptionist said that she would be sure to send a mobile unit as quickly as possible. Well, the 'mobile unit' took a while coming, and I was a bit surprised because the distance was very short. When the 'mobile unit' arrived, it turned out to be PC Ross on his bike, complete with his bicycle clips! PC Ross became a trusty colleague; whenever we needed him, he was always there. He knew the names of the pupils and used what I now know to be football references like, 'I've marked your card', when admonishing offenders. He was teased unmercifully by the kids, because, if I remember correctly, he had very red hair, that you could see peeking out from under his helmet and rather prominent sticky-out front teeth. He did look rather similar to Postman Pat. Teased? Yes, but respected in equal measure.

There was a crime that I remember well, which didn't take much solving. One of the younger boys, it would appear, had been doing something he shouldn't do and his 'friends' had reported to me that they thought he'd been taking milk from the doorstep of one of the neighbouring houses, so I summoned the young man to interview him. He came into my room looking suitably solemn and before I had a chance to say anything, he piped up, "Madam, I don't care what my mates say, I don't know anything about Rodney's bike." Now that one wasn't too tricky, was it?

The best crime story of all, however, concerned the local pub, a rather well-heeled pub where the fairly middle-class parents of the catchment area that my school was in, had pleasant evenings and pleasant lunches. One day a very big, smart police car drove up the drive which was immediately outside the window of my office and out climbed two very smart young police officers, who were shown into my room. They wished to interview two of my senior pupils. I was not keen for that to happen, because there wasn't a parent present, and I didn't know what the interview was going to involve; so, I asked the police officers to explain the problem. The problem was that these two boys had stolen the condom machine from the public lavatories in the aforementioned hostelry and had fastened it to a tree in Goose Fair. Goose Fair is a very big annual event in the social calendar of Nottingham, where hundreds of young, and not so young, people gather every late afternoon, evening and into the night, for most of a week, with the sole intention of having fun. Trying to keep my face straight, I asked the police officers, whether they had come to arrest my boys for the theft or commend the boys for their act of public service. One of the policemen had a sense of humour and grinned. The other one had better control of his face muscles, or no sense of humour, because he didn't appear to find my remark humorous at all.

We went round and round the mill for a bit, until eventually, I said to them, "Let us cut to the chase. Is the publican intending to charge my boys or not?"

There was a pause, then one policeman looked at the other one, and they said in unison, "No madam, he is not going to press charges."

I said, "Why is that?" and the policeman with a sense of humour, gave a grin and said, "Because, madam, when the condom machine was returned to the pub, there was a lot more money in it than there had been when it was taken."

Another occasion, when there was a problem, it concerned a young man who had been, it would seem, glue-sniffing. It was at a time when glue-sniffing was prevalent. He was a senior pupil and my big, black, deputy and I decided we would interview him together, so we summoned him. He duly came to my office, and we went through, solemnly, the problems of glue-sniffing; the fact that it could be a trigger leading to other drugs and that it really was something to be avoided. Now the substance that he had been sniffing wasn't specifically, actually, glue, it was something that, I was told, was called Liquid Gold. Now, I knew what Liquid Gold was, without any doubt. It was an aromatic oil that I bought in a tin and rubbed, from time to time, into my teak furniture to enhance the appearance of the surface. My deputy, a rugby player, said he knew what Liquid Gold was. It was a spray, an analgesic spray, that the trainer would use if a rugby player or a football player was injured on the pitch and the injury was a muscular injury because spraying it on the said muscle would give very quick relief to the pain. Neither of us had bothered to share with the other person what we believed Liquid Gold to be, and we were laying it on a bit. Until, in the end, the young man, with some exasperation, said, "I don't know what you're making such a fuss about. It came from the sex shop, and I only used it for the purpose for which it is intended."

My deputy and I didn't dare look at each other, and I think it was me who said, "Then what purpose was it intended for?"

Whereupon the young man, in the most dignified manner, that he could muster, said "It is bought to spray into the air because it enhances, intensifies and prolongs the pleasure experienced when having sexual intercourse."

Well, my deputy and I were aghast, and my deputy had the control to say, through gritted teeth, "Do you think you could go out into the corridor so we can discuss this alone, for a moment?"

The boy got up and went out and the pair of us fell about with laughter. Unfortunately, the wall between my office and the corridor was, pretty much, paper-thin and so, the young man in question, would have heard us laughing heartily. We summoned him back and, as he was over the age of sixteen, we went through a token admonition about sexual responsibilities, etc., but I don't think, after our obvious hilarity, we could convey very much conviction. Some of the staff, of course, had heard us roaring with laughter, when we were supposed to be dealing with the pupil severely, and we had to offer some explanation. So, what we did was pin on the wall of staff room a list, asking the staff to put on the list what they believed Liquid Gold to be. We got no less than nine alternative suggestions and each of us had the title of the thing we were describing slightly wrong. Someone said it was the high-interest account that the bank offered; someone said it was what he sprayed on his tongue when he didn't want his wife to know he'd been smoking. I wonder what your answer would be, if you were asked, just on the spot, to say what Liquid Gold is.

The police, when we did need them, were very supportive and on one occasion, there was a bomb scare. We had phone calls purporting to be bomb scares on more than one occasion, but, only on one occasion did my secretary, who took the call, think that it might be genuine. So, we phoned the police immediately and they said they would send an officer, and in the meanwhile, we should evacuate the school. Well fortunately, on our site there was a junior school and an infant school and the headteachers of those two schools gave refuge to our pupils, in their buildings while the police came to find the bomb. When the police vehicle came it was a big white van. The back door of it opened and out jumped a very aggressive-looking woman, who had more accoutrements strapped to her uniform than, I think, I'd ever seen before. She was accompanied by an extremely large and fierce-looking Alsatian and she said to me,

"Where's the armed intruder?" and I said, "There isn't an armed intruder. It's a bomb scare." Whereupon she summoned her snarling, bristling Alsatian back to her side, pushed it back into the van and said to me, disparagingly, "My dog doesn't sniff!"

There wasn't a bomb, I'm pleased to say. I'll tell you some other stories another day. Bye-bye!

4. Examinations and Exchanges

Hello everyone. One of the few people I know to be promoted after they had officially retired was my husband, Peter, who spent the last few years of his formal working life teaching pupils with special educational needs. On one occasion, he came to help out at the school where I was headteacher because our regular special-needs teacher had been taken ill. Now, we had in the school, a young girl called Ebony and she was very black. She was an able girl, socially worldly-wise and confident but she had literacy problems and so we employed a special-needs teacher to come to some of her lessons to help her access them fully. On one such occasion it was a library lesson, and my husband was the teacher that was there to help her. Before the lesson began, while they were getting their papers and things together, Ebony told Peter, in a very cheerful way, that she was very happy because her cousin Leticia had joined the school. She and Leticia were good friends and so it was very nice that they were now pupils together. Just at that moment, a class of young girls came out of the school changing rooms and ran past the library window on their way to their lesson on the playing field.

Ebony said, with great excitement, "Oh look, look! There's Leticia."

My husband looked up and said, innocently, "Which one?"

Whereupon Ebony gave Peter a somewhat withering glance and said, "Oh come on, sir, the black one!"

Most of this part of my talk is going to be snippets — one-liners, you might say, but I'm going to tell you a few stories which are a bit longer than that. Some girls are middle-aged from a very early age and that's a very useful thing. They are the people who make sure things work smoothly, who are organised, who like organising and, dare I say, mothering other people. My school had a fair share of those. A date in my diary was causing a problem because the district had a new area education officer, who had booked an appointment to come and see me for an introduction to the school. It was also a regular event that we should once a year have the saga of the school photographs and my gosh! What a saga it was! The photographer wished to come on the same day as the area education officer and, for a while, I thought I was going to have to cancel one or the other. Then it occurred to me that I could use a group of my pupils to put together all of the official business for the school photographs and I gathered together a group of earnest young women to do just that. They set up a booth for the photographer; they produced endless lists of which class was going to come, at what time; which teacher was going to supervise them, and where siblings were going to have their photographs together even though they weren't in the same year and how that was going to be arranged, etc. They discussed it all with me and it all seemed scrupulously planned. On the day, I sat in my office hoping that the school photographs were going smoothly and waiting for the area education officer. Until, worried that nothing was happening, I thought I better go on a recce, so I went to my secretary, and I asked, "Has the education officer arrived? and she replied, "Not to my knowledge, madam."

"Oh dear!" I said, "Well, if he comes while I'm not in my office, tell him I'm just checking on the arrangements for the school photographs."

I went down to the quiet area at the back of the school hall where the photographer was to have his booth, and all seemed to be under control.

One of the senior girls came and said to me, "Madam, we're all ready, but I'm a bit worried because the photographer doesn't seem very clear about what he's going to be doing and, what's more, he doesn't seem to have any equipment."

So, I went up to the gentlemen concerned, greeted him happily and said, "Everything under control?"

He waved at me a sheaf of papers and said, "Your girls have provided me with all this; I've no idea what they're on about and they won't let me get word in sideways."

I then said, "Excuse me! You are the school photographer, aren't you?"

He said, "School photographer? Rubbish! I am the new education officer."

You can't win them all can you? I am pleased to say that, as the day wore on, the photographer did materialise, the photographs turned out fine, and the education officer went away with quite a positive impression about how well my senior girls could organise something.

Exams. Secondary schools, even before league tables, were always preoccupied and dominated by exams. Exams brought with them their own set of problems, public exams particularly. In these days, when we're all having to socially isolate, etc., having to stay a metre apart is a new bit of legislation, but it was legislated for examination desks all those years ago. I had an exam officer, a splendid gentleman, but you could always tell his state of mind by how vertical his hair was, because as he got more and more agitated, if something was going wrong, he would run his fingers through his hair, until his hair stood up quite vertically. In the fullness of time, an exam appeared on the curriculum, which was computer studies. Nobody, I think, does that as a separate subject any more; using a computer is part of the modus operandi of everybody's life. The computer studies exam was, thanks to somebody's wisdom, set to be on the same day as the main maths exam for all of the examination year group. So, we required, in the entrance hall and the main school hall which were linked with each other, to have, ninety desks for the maths exam and nine desks for the computer studies group. I, several times, I'm sorry to say, said to my Exam Officer, "Now, don't forget the extra nine desks on the day of the maths exam."

Unbeknownst to me, the head of maths had also said, "Don't forget the extra nine desks on the day of the maths exam and the chap who taught computer studies had said, "Don't forget I need nine desks for the computer studies exam."

Come the day, all the pupils were closeted behind closed doors, waiting for the moment when they could go in, sit down and start to open and read their papers. Everyone was nervous, a huge number of people, somewhat agitated. The doors to the main hall were thrown open and there, in splendid, isolated glory, in the vast room, were nine desks. The exam officer had not forgotten the nine desks; he'd been reminded so many times, he had forgotten the ninety! If you've ever seen pictures of worker ants, you would get an impression of what happened when ninety exam desks, or any other desks that were around, had to be gathered, set out, measured, with seats, in a very limited amount of time. The papers had to be opened within thirty minutes of the exam room being available. Both exams did go ahead, and I thought my deputy head was going to take off, because his hair was so very vertical.

There was also an occasion, when one of my pupils was ill in hospital, long-term ill in hospital, and it was arranged that he would do his examination in the hospital ward. I was going to take the exam papers, still sealed, from the school to the hospital, where the sister in charge of the ward would be there to receive them. The hospital in question is vast and the ability to park there is almost nil; it is a horror story, rather than a legend, in its lifetime. I got there, and drove round and round and, although I knew where the ward was, which door to go into, parking anywhere near was impossible. This was partly because, the area immediately outside the convenient door was a building site, where additional building work was going on. I parked my car in the middle of the chaos, and then I leaned over and took from the back seat a clipboard and a hard hat. They were both there because of work that I had been doing in the theatre; when you're putting up scenery, the official regulations are that you wear a hard hat. I clipped the exam papers to the clipboard, put on the hard hat, and brazenly walked past the workmen, wishing them a good morning and hoping their day was going to go well. I went up to the ward, where I delivered the exam papers. I came back; I gave a similar greeting to the workmen, who cheerfully said, "Cheerio!" I got back in my car and drove off. Bluff is sometimes a wonderful thing.

Talking of the theatre, how about this one? I was taking a whole year group dance practice in the school hall prior to pupils being chosen to be in the next school production. I wasn't going to be directing the production, but I had volunteered to help in this way. I was teaching the children a step which went: step, close, step, stamp, step, close, step, stamp, but I said, enthusiastically: "Step close, step Bonk, step close, step Bonk."

One of my senior boys, tapped me on the shoulder and said, very graciously, "Excuse me Madam! If I were you, I would say, Step stamp, rather than, Step bonk. I will explain later."

Who says that the age of gallantry is dead?

I'm going to leave the last word with someone you will have heard of. I was at a conference, it was in the middle of the summer, but the air conditioning had been on so powerfully that, although the men in the room might have been fairly comfortable, women, in summer dresses, were frozen. It was very near lunchtime; my middle was beginning to rumble, and I know I had allowed my attention to wander. One of the people at the meeting was our former Prime Minister, Tony Blair. When he was making his concluding remarks, he said, to all and sundry, "Well, I have to say, I agree with Jean Gemmell."

I sent up a silent prayer, *Please, don't let him ask me to amplify.*

I had no idea then, and I have no idea now, what he was talking about. I'm not sure I ever agreed with Tony Blair. Thank you so much for listening to me. Bye-bye!

A Stranger in a Strange Land

1. To the Strange Land

When I decided to do this new talk, one of the first things that came to mind was the title: *A Stranger in a Strange Land.* I thought this title sounded as though it might have come from something like *Fiddler on the Roof,* and was surprised to find, when I looked it up, that it is actually biblical.

Not a very strange land, you understand, because it was Scotland, but it wasn't on a day trip to Edinburgh or a quick visit to Glasgow, it was where I lived for the first four years of my married life, in Thurso. Thurso is in Caithness. Caithness is the most northerly county on the mainland of Great Britain and Dunnet Head, on the Caithness coast, is the most northerly point on the mainland of Great Britain. And what was up there? Dounreay, an Atomic Energy Authority establishment.

I was married on the 30th of December, that was four days later than Boxing Day as had been planned, because on Christmas Eve the vicar's son had fallen off his motorbike on the ice and had broken his neck. I can tell you about that now, quite cheerfully, because, fortunately, the young man made a complete recovery, but of course, at the time, no one knew that would be so.

Thus, the wedding was postponed. The new plan was fairly simple, my fiancé and I would be married on the 30th of December; we would go to London on New Year's Eve, to pay a visit to a much-loved aunt in hospital and I would take to her, as a gift, my wedding bouquet. We would then set off in our car to Thurso, where I was going to live. At that time, I was teaching in a girls' boarding school in St Neots and my new husband had already been working at the Atomic Energy establishment for some months. What we didn't recognise, was that the weather was not in our favour.

There is a very famous poem that comes to mind about a long journey undertaken in the dead of winter described in words far more eloquent and elegant than mine. A Christmas journey made at the worst time of year for such an undertaking. Well, we weren't wise men following a star seeking to find the Christ Child, we were merely newly-weds trying to follow a map — 1961 was long before Sat-Navs — seeking the town that was to be our first home together. The travellers in the poem had transport problems and so did we — their camels were *recalcitrant* or was it *refractory,* our car was old rickety and noisy and, worst of all, had no heater. When we got to London the world was covered in snow. We found our aunt in the hospital, and being New Year's Eve, everyone was quite festive; they made us welcome, and she was delighted to see us. We stayed too long and by the time we left, it was snowing again. New Year's Eve in London, in the dark, in a snowstorm! Undaunted, we set off on the journey to Thurso — a town which I had never, in my life, ever seen, or visited. The plan was that the journey would take a couple of days, leaving about a week for "our honeymoon" in our new home, until I needed to go back to the boarding school to serve out a term's notice before I went to Thurso to stay. The journey did not work out as planned, it was something of a nightmare. The roads getting out of London were terrible — in fact, all the roads were terrible and everywhere was blocked. The snow got worse and worse as the journey went on.. The estimated two-day journey lasted virtually a week and, starting somewhere around about Aberdeen, I had tonsillitis! Whenever I'm very hungry, a vision of steak and chips with grilled tomato and salad floats before my eyes, because it was the meal that the hotel — I've no idea which hotel — served in Aberdeen. It looked and smelled wonderful, but my throat hurt so much, that hunger notwithstanding, I could not eat a single morsel.

We continued on the journey. The weather was relentless. Before you arrive in Caithness you have to drive across a moor which is about seventeen miles wide, it's called the Claise Moire. All you could see in the gloom was snow. The only way you knew where the road was, was because there were little poles, with things like upturned table tennis bats on the top of them, to give you some indication as to whether you were on the road or not. I became more and more convinced that I was going to a place where the people lived in igloos and where habitation, as I knew it, did not exist. I have to say now, I have never been so relieved and happy in my life, as when we went over a slight rise in the ground and there below us, I could see a river and beyond the river, over a perfectly solid-looking stone bridge, a little town, with a church and with buildings, and even though it was still in what seemed to be perpetual gloom, snow. Had there been a few twinkling lights, it might have made a good scene for a Christmas card. And thus, I arrived in the strange land, a stranger in a strange land.

When I got there and began to live there, Thurso was actually much more fun than I anticipated. We spent the few days staying with some friends that my husband had made in the months that he'd been there, while I was not; they made us very welcome. I enjoyed the very brief period that was supposedly my honeymoon before I caught the all-night sleeper back to London. There to change trains and go back to Huntingdonshire, to the boarding school where I taught. The night on the sleeper was something of a nightmare too, because, immediately after the New Year, with people going back to their various places of employment in the south part of Scotland or in England, the train was very full and there were no bunks available, so it was a sit-up'all-night journey. I can't remember how many times the train stopped, it was a good few and although there were no refreshments available on the train, I think I felt as if I was floating on a sea of strong tea by the time we arrived in London. This was because the other people in the carriage, all men, had been very welcoming, very friendly and insisted on leaping off and buying me tea and biscuits every time the train stopped. There was one snag: I wasn't brave enough to tell them I don't like tea.

Surprisingly, I enjoyed being back at school, because there was something of a cachet about being a new bride in a girls' boarding school. The girls thought it was all very exciting and very romantic, especially when it came to Valentine's Day. It was tradition in the school, that although the staff had their own table, they ate in the same dining room as the pupils. So, on the morning of 14th February, we were all in the dining room for breakfast and in came the Bursar with various cards, which were delivered to the girls, with great excitement, and for me, there was a card and a quite large squidgy parcel.

Everyone said: "Oh, open it! Open it!"

The postmark indicated that it had come from the north of Scotland, presumably from my new husband. I opened what I assumed would be a romantic and loving present but out fell a pair of trousers, which had definitely seen better days, and a note, which was somewhat succinct. It said, *Dear Jean, Will you please put a new pocket in these trousers, because one of the pockets has a hole that's been mended many times already. Much love.*

I was mortified! My colleagues thought it amusing, and the girls thought it hilarious. But never mind, at least I knew that my new husband was alive and well and had some degree of care about his sartorial appearance. The end of term, of course, duly arrived and I returned to Caithness, but not to what I had hoped would be my new home, one of the new houses that the Atomic Energy Authority had built for the influx of young people, who had come from the universities of Great Britain to man Dounreay. Sadly, I hadn't realised that one didn't even get on the list for such an allocation of a house, until one was married. So, we had only been on the list since I arrived there briefly in January and no such house was yet available. But my husband had managed to find us a little rented house, which was right in the middle of the town of Thurso and that was where we spent the first months of our marriage. The next parts of my story will relate to living there. I'll tell you those tomorrow. Bye-bye.

2. The Shock of the New

If you studied Latin at 'O 'level, as I did, you might remember that one of the set books was Caesar's *Gallic Wars* and the opening sentence was: "The whole of Gaul is divided into three parts." Well, if it was true of Gaul, it was also true of Thurso. At least it was with regards to the population: the tourists, transient; the locals, long established; the 'Atomics' imported, and I was one of the 'Atomics'. You may remember that my journey to Thurso, the first time I ever went there, the first time I ever saw the town, had been very much a pain. I am delighted to report that, when I finally arrived there, I found that being in Thurso was a pleasure. Everyone was very welcoming; it was almost as if the people had been waiting for me. Since I was a new wife, in one case hopefully, that was actually true. There was so much to do. There were clubs, societies and sports to be involved in and individual friendships to make and bond. In fact, it was a bit like going to a different university, because so many of the young people there, who had come to work at the Atomic Energy Authority, had come, pretty much, straight from university. I very quickly felt at home.

And home? Well, home was a house, or rather half a house, that my husband had rented and had been living in while I was still at the boarding school. It was a rather quirky house; the front door opened directly onto the pavement. When you went in the front door, to the right, there was a staircase, to the left, a door into the only downstairs room and opposite the front door a blank wall. If you looked very carefully, there were slight clues that, once upon a time, there had been a door there as well. The downstairs room was big, it had a sink under the kitchen window and the window was, like the front door, right onto the pavement. There was a gas stove, a gas boiler and the weirdest gas clothes dryer I have ever seen, before or since. It certainly worked and the clothes got dry, but anything that came out of it, came out as stiff and as rigid as if it were made of cardboard. There was also a table and some chairs. Going up the stairs there was a very cosy, somewhat Edwardian sitting room, with lots of comfy furniture and lots of bric-a-brac, soft furnishings and cushions and an open fireplace to have, in the winter months, an open fire. The window was right onto the road and the road looked across to a little square. Every Saturday night, after I'd lived there for a while, I was terrified that I was going to be lynched, because the town pipe band would parade in the little square and play the pipes. Now I'm very fond of the sound of bagpipes and so, I think, was my husband, but the very first time we heard the band coming down the road, he threw up the window, a sash window, put his head through and called out: "Och aye, the Jocks are coming!"

I was pretty cross. I said that it was rude, and we didn't want to make any problems between us and the neighbours. He thought it was funny and, the more I protested, the more determined he was that he would greet the pipe band in this manner every week. I am pleased to say that, if people did hear, they accepted it as a greeting and not as anything pejorative. That's exactly the way referring to us as, 'the Atomics', was received. It was never considered to be rude; it was always accepted to be just a statement of fact.

There was also a little bedroom with a large and comfortable double bed; the slight problem there was that the bed took up most of the available space. The room had one window which overlooked a garden, a long, thin, vastly overgrown garden with evidence that there had once been a path from the house to a different street, which was at the bottom of the garden. We never found a route from the house into that garden or actually the end on the road which then led back to the house. Why it had been boarded up or at what point in the past, was always a mystery. And then there was the lavatory with a fairly generous wash basin and its own gas water heater — one of those water heaters, where you turn on the tap and you hope the pilot light is working and you press the button for the gas and after a little while there is the sort of bang that makes you jump out of your skin and the water begins to become warm. I must have used that little geyser many times a day for all the months we lived there. I never got used to the bang. I always knew it was going to happen and it never indicated anything untoward, except a loud noise but it always made me jump. Have you noticed the problem? Yes, there was a problem. There was no bath and there was no shower. There was a third floor, and you could go upstairs to the third floor and there you would come across two large rooms that were empty and when I say empty, I mean empty. How were we to cope with our ablutions? Well on a day-to-day basis one could, as it were, wash on the instalment plan, but we had made friends with the people that we originally stayed with when we were on our rather shortened honeymoon. They were keen bridge players; my husband was a keen bridge player, and I was a vaguely competent bridge player. So, a ritual was quickly established that once a week we would visit our friends for bridge and bath. It all seemed to work fine if a bit unorthodox.

One of the problems that did however occur was that I hadn't been north of the border for very long before I started to experience symptoms like extreme hay fever, itchy eyes, runny nose, sneezing, swelling of the face and such. I went to the doctor. When I got to the doctor's, bearing in mind I'd never been before, I discovered that I already was quite friendly with the man because we were of similar age, and I had joined the choral society and he sang in the choral society. I explained my symptoms and that I didn't really think it was hay fever and he asked, in a lovely Scottish accent, which I won't attempt to mimic, if I had done anything different in the last weeks or months. I grinned and said, well, I was living in a different country, I was living in a different house, I was married to a new husband, I had a new job and he said, "Oh don't go on!" Although the information was helpful it was rather difficult to actually tie down which of those changes had brought about my symptoms.

At this point, I thought there was one thing that wasn't new and that I wasn't keen to be new and that reminded me that many of the young women who came to live in Thurso — especially newly married ones like me — were taunted with the fact that the particular nuclear reactor at Dounreay was called a 'fast breeder' reactor and fast breeding was not part of my plan. So, the doctor explained to me that the contraceptive of choice at that time was the pill; new, adventurous and somewhat controversial in some camps, and he was sure however that I was the sort of girl who would cope with that. And I was pretty sure I was too. And so, I was duly given a prescription to take the pill. Some weeks later, I went to see the doctor again, having seen him every week at the choral society anyway, and he asked me how my hay fever symptoms are. Unfortunately, they were pretty much the same, not worse, but pretty much the same, and then he said, "And how are you getting on with the pill?" And I said, "Ah, well! I haven't taken it."

To which he replied, "Och, Jeanie, don't say you're scared."

"No", said I, "I'm not scared, I'm pregnant."

At that point he forgot that he was my doctor and, remembered that he was my friend, and, as a friend would, he roared with laughter and said something, which, in spite of the Scottish accent, sounded remarkably like, "Too late! Ho-Ho!"

I'll tell you some more soon. Bye-bye.

3. Testing, testing

Good evening. There were two things I had resolved to deal with as soon as I was ensconced in my new home in Thurso and neither of them involved starting a family. The two things were that I needed to find myself a job and I needed to pass my driving test. Finding myself a job wasn't very tricky: there were two high schools to hand, one in Thurso and the other in Wick. Thurso High School didn't have a vacancy for a teacher of maths or physics at that time, but Wick High School did. I think it was probably cover for a long-term absence or something like that, so I got myself a job there quickly. When I told my new-found friends in Thurso that I was going to work in Wick, I was a bit surprised at the cool reception that the news received. In fact, one of the people actually said, "Och! You'll not understand the Wickers."

I thought, how foolish, I can understand the people of Thurso, the Highland accent is very attractive and not at all difficult to follow. Little did I know that the Thurso accent is very different from the one I was going to encounter. I also discovered the reason for the cool reception of my news. Although the two towns are actually quite close together, not much further apart than Derby and Nottingham, the two towns are not, as it were, well inclined towards one another, or at least they were not all those years ago. I never really understood the reason, but I did evolve a theory. I think it was to do with economics; the towns had never been prosperous at the same time. For years and years, Thurso did well from sheep farming until the big cotton mills of the Midlands started to flourish and cotton took over in popularity from wool. Then, it was the fishing industry in Wick that was bringing in the money. When the fishing industry faded, partly because of much regulation of where you could fish and how much you could fish, it was Thurso that became prosperous again, because, at about that time, the Atomic Energy Authority built the nuclear reactor at Dounreay. I don't know how things are now, but I do know that there was a tangibly frosty relationship then.

When I started to teach at Wick High School, I was sorry to discover that whoever had said I would find the Wick accent hard to follow was right. The Wick accent was derived from the countries of the north, the other fishing countries, the Scandinavian countries, especially Norway. And it was only then, that it began to dawn on me, that the gloom I talked about when describing my week-long journey to the north of Scotland — that all-pervading gloom of my first arrival in Thurso, was because Thurso is nearer to the Arctic Circle than it is to London and in the winter months, there is little if any daylight and in the summertime virtually no night. When I was there, a cricket match was played on the night of the Summer Solstice, because it never really got dark.

I was welcomed into the staff room and officially became a member of the teaching fraternity at Wick High School when I was presented with a "tawse". You may not be familiar with what a tawse is; I certainly wasn't. It's a leather object, a strap with the leather on one end split in to several thongs; the idea is that, if necessary, one keeps discipline by whacking a pupil with it! I was appalled and am pleased to say that in the time that I taught at Wick High School, which was not as long as intended, I never used it. The language was difficult for me; not so difficult for the pupils because they were used to hearing English voices on the radio, though every time I said the word 'graph', I was teased and the pupils chuckled, and I'm sorry to say that that didn't stop when I came to the Midlands. The long 'a' for 'grass' and 'graph' which is part of my diction has never gone away, in spite of having now lived many more years north of Watford than I ever lived south of it. One day I was about to take the register — that was a pretty boring activity, because so many of the names in the register were the same: Munro, and occasionally Sinclair. There were one or two other names of course. Historically, or so I was told, Munro was the name of the peasantry and Sinclair was the name of the gentry — or at least those that were better-off. We had a new girl join the class and her surname was McPhee. I didn't understand why she was not made welcome by the rest of the pupils. In fact, it seemed to me that they avoided her, which was very strange, because she was a charming, outgoing, sunny girl. I didn't understand, until someone explained to me that the name McPhee, in that part of the world is associated with the Tinkers and the Tinkers were deemed to be idlers who weren't very honest. I am delighted to say that the sunny nature that she displayed, and her own personality quite quickly worked through that prejudice.

So, I'm about to start a lesson and it's after break and one of the pupils is not there. I said to his mate, "What's happened to Andy?" or whatever his name actually was.

The boy replied, "Och wheel, he's picked his pinkie on a perd and he's cronin," and he had! Stung his hand (or pinky finger) on a thistle and was crying. I know that now, but I didn't know that then.

So, I had a job, and all I had to do next was to pass my driving test. I'd had some lessons from a driving school when I was teaching in St Neots, so I wasn't completely hopeless behind the wheel. One of the places where, in the evening, I could practise driving, was a vast open space near the reactor at the Atomic Energy Station. It was the Staff Bus Park. If anyone had any doubt that living near a nuclear reactor could be deemed to be dangerous, you only had to see the buses — enough buses to take every member of the staff on the site away at a moment's notice — to realise the enormity of the things that could go wrong. The buses were there all day and every day, and the drivers were in them all the time. However, in the early evening, when most of the staff had gone home, the car park was pretty empty and that's when I could practise my driving. Taking a driving test in Thurso was not really as unpredictable as it might be in any other town, because there was, for instance, only one crossroads where there was a halt sign on the road; there was only one place where there were traffic lights; there was no lane driving at all and I don't actually remember that there were any roundabouts, so you would think I would manage to pass my test. I didn't, however, actually pass until the third attempt, although interestingly, I only failed my test once. How can that be?

Well, it was like this: on the first occasion, I'm in the car, I'm taking my test, I think everything is going quite smoothly and I'm about to drive over the main bridge out of Thurso town centre, and there, standing in the middle of the road is a policeman, who lifts his hand with his palm towards me. I thought he was just giving a friendly gesture that I acknowledged in like style and drove straight past. Only then, did it occur to me that, although there was hardly any traffic about that day, there was rather a crowd of people on the pavement at the side of the road, giving their attention to a large black limousine sporting a very heraldic-looking little flag on the bonnet, that was driving towards me. The Queen Mother owned the Castle of Mey, near to the town and had chosen that day and that time to arrive in Thurso, via the bridge, for a visit. No comment was made until the end of the test, when the examiner said that I had failed my test, because I had not obeyed an official instruction from the policeman: to halt. I would have done so, though, had I realised it was an official instruction.

The second occasion when I tried again to pass my test, was when I was very pregnant and therefore rather large. The test was going quite well again, until the tester asked to me, in a conversational manner, "Is your baby due soon?" and I replied ingenuously, "Oh, about a fortnight ago."

At which point the tester took the immediate decision to abandon the test on health and safety grounds, because to attempt an emergency stop was not recommended under the circumstances! So, you see, I didn't pass that test either, but neither did I fail it. I had nearly achieved both of my objectives and I'll tell you about what happened thereafter in my next chat.

4. Nativity

Hello! On Christmas day 1962, seven young couples sat down to enjoy their Christmas lunch at one of the Thurso hotels. At some point during the meal, when one of the ladies in the group left the table, the waiter said to the rest of the assembled company, "Is Madam coming back?"

The waiter must have been surprised, because the response to the question was that most of the people around the table tittered or sniggered and one voice said, "I hope so."

The person who left the table was me and I only left the table to go to the powder room. The person who hoped I was coming back was my husband, and the reason for the amusement was that my son — I didn't know then of course that it was a son — was due to be born on Christmas Day. As it happened, he wasn't born on Christmas Day; he didn't make his arrival into the world until three weeks later!

My pregnancy, I'm delighted to say, had gone remarkably smoothly. Working at Wick High School had kept me busy, but I had still found time to sing with the choral society and direct a production of a play called *Dinner With The Family*'at Thurso Town Hall for the local dramatic society. I had also made innumerable sandwiches, as I was a keen supporter and devoted follower of Dounreay Badminton Club, Thurso Badminton Club and Caithness County Badminton Club. Many of the players were the same people and one of those people was my talented sportsman husband. As it happened, our son finally decided to make an entrance on an occasion which was not the best timing in the world, because the badminton club — I don't remember which one, was playing away. I think they were playing at a place called Dingwall and I had gone with Tom in order to watch the match. Tom, by the way, was my husband, I don't think I've mentioned his name hitherto.

At some point during the proceedings, I became pretty convinced that I shouldn't be sitting in a badminton hall enjoying the game, I should be reporting to the hospital maternity unit because '"things were beginning to happen'. Eventually, I managed to attract my husband's attention when he was not actually playing. He hastily got the car, and I was bundled into it with a chorus of good wishes from all of the players and the rest of the people there on that evening, ringing in my ears. We drove back to Thurso, and I was duly — dare I say — delivered, to Dunbar Hospital. Deposited might be more appropriate word because, in those days men didn't tend to stay and be present during the birth of a child and my husband still had a couple of games to play in the match, which was a training match, and much of the outcome depended on his success on the court. so having made sure that I was well looked after and comfortable (?) he went back to the badminton.

My son took a long time to arrive; I'm told that 24 hours is not actually that long for the delivery of a first child, but it seemed pretty long to me. I'm also told that it is not unusual for women in extremes of pain and distress to curse and swear while having a child. I was no exception, but I was teased by the midwives, after the event was all over, because the only expletive that I had used during the process of childbirth was, "Gosh!" They thought it was terribly English stiff upper lip. The fact was that I had actually used the word several hundred times, notwithstanding nothing still seemed to be happening. The midwife who was caring for me, very carefully, was short of stature and in order for her to see what she was doing, she had a little platform on which she could stand, in the labour ward, so that she was high enough to have an appropriate view of her patient. The little platform was painted white in recognition of its position in a sterile room, but it really could have done with another coat of white paint. I was already suspicious that it looked like the size and shape of an orange box, when I noticed that through the paint, I could still read the word 'Outspan'. Even in my somewhat preoccupied state, I was amused. When the process of dilation had gone on for a long time and the midwife was sure the child was about to arrive, she kept encouraging me, by saying, "We're nearly there. We're nearly there. I can see the head."

Then, suddenly she said, producing from somewhere in her uniform a fairly ordinary looking pair of scissors, "Och, woman, ye have no elasticity." At which point, with a couple of enthusiastic and appropriate snips, generating a deal of blood and a fair bit of yelling on the part of my lusty son, suddenly, there I was, a mother of a very healthy and energetic little boy. I was given the child to hug, being assured that the blood was mine and not the baby's and then my son was whisked away to be 'tidied up'. The tidying up involved trimming his mass of hair and also trimming his tiny fingernails and toenails which were so long they were likely to do either him or me injury. Thereupon, the midwife set to, to sew up where she had cut. Later on, that night my friend the doctor arrived to see me. He congratulated me on the birth of a healthy child, he congratulated my husband on being a father and then, having examined the midwife's handiwork, he said "Och, that woman is far better with a needle than I am," and then he confessed that the reason he'd not been present at any point during the proceedings was that he had been at a Sea Cadets committee meeting! I've failed to mention that at that time the Dunbar Hospital had a permanent staff of nurses but the doctors that served it were the GPs of the town.

I'm not normally of a very nervous disposition, but I was pretty nervous when I took my new baby home from the hospital for the first time. As we went in to the little house that we lived in, I was something of a quiver. I had never taken an interest in small children; I had never thought I was maternal. I had never nursed a child, changed a child or even for that matter pushed a pram and this scrap of humanity was there, with me to make sure that he lived a healthy, happy life and I wasn't sure that I knew how to do that. Many, many, years later, when my son, a highly successful businessman, was at an adult dinner party where I was also a guest, somebody asked him what my style as a mother had been like. He grinned and said, "Appropriate chastisement and loving neglect."

I'm not sure that I recommend that to you as a form of childcare, but since he's done pretty well for himself in his life, I must have got something right. I'll tell you some more another day. Bye-bye.

5. Flying High

Hello! For the first six months after my son was born, I was pretty much a home mum, trying to learn, on the job, how to be a housewife and a good mother to a tiny new baby. The whole enterprise wasn't as traumatic as I had anticipated it to be, partly because I had the support of a pretty hands-on husband but most particularly because I was lucky enough to have given birth to a child, who in general, was amiable, tolerant, and cheerful. Also, although he'd taken a long time to decide to come into the world, having got there, he was absolutely fascinated, from the word go, by everything that was going on around him and particularly by the people that populated this strange new place.

I wonder if any of you have ever flown in a Dakota. I mention this, because the other thing that helped in those early months of new motherhood was that my own mother was a very brave woman. She'd never flown in an aeroplane ever, but decided that she would come on her own, by air, to Thurso, partly to support me, but partly, of course, to see her first grandchild. Now the Atomic Energy Authority had at that time, a fleet of Dakotas. They were used, sometimes to move freight from one station to another, sometimes for staff to go for a meeting or special event or off-site work and, sometimes, if there was room on a plane, one could have a seat to go to the south of Scotland or into England in order to make social visits. My mother was lucky enough to get such a seat to come from the South of England, where she lived, to visit her new grandson and family in Thurso. If you've never been on a Dakota, take it from me, sixty years ago it was quite an interesting experience. A small aeroplane with seats for about ten passengers, sometimes fewer, depending on whether or not there is freight as well. The back wheels of the plane are quite small, and the front wheels are very big, so that when the plane is on the ground, the fuselage is at a somewhat alarming angle to the horizontal. Passengers get onto the plane through the door, which is at the rear of the plane, i.e., near the back wheels. Having got on, it's a bit like climbing up the north face of the Eiger to get to the seats at the front. My little boy had his very first experience of being in an aeroplane on a Dakota. The plane is sturdy and reliable but not given to too many refinements; its stabilisers aren't great — or perhaps even non-existent and if you're in a Dakota in turbulent weather it tends to roll and to bounce. On the very first occasion when this little boy, who would only have been about six months old, was on a Dakota, it was lunch time. The passengers had been provided with a somewhat perfunctory packed lunch and my son had a pot of baby food, ''Baby apples', which I had brought with me — he loved ''Baby apples'. The plane hit turbulence and was bouncing around all over the place. Most of the passengers were looking a bit green and very nervous — not remotely interested in the thought of eating any food — while my small son was bouncing up and down on my lap chortling with glee every time the plane bounced and munching his 'baby apples' with great gusto. I'm sure he thought that the advent of turbulence on that journey was put on especially for his entertainment.

Now, the Dounreay fast breeder reactor had lived up to its name and although I was the one who led the charge, as it were, when it came to babies, the group of girls (women?) that I was close friends with, seven of us, had produced several fairly quickly. My house, the little rented house, was quite near to the shops and we girls took it upon ourselves to agree to have Friday morning as our main shopping morning. In the middle of our shopping chores, we would always stop and go to The Royal Hotel which had a big foyer with a coffee lounge area for our 'elevenses'. We, with our various offspring, would gather for coffee, a bun, and a natter. If the babies were awake or fractious, we would bring them into the lounge with us. Everyone seemed pretty tolerant of their presence; if the weather was nice or the babies were asleep, we would leave them in their prams in a line outside the front door. It says much for the times I describe that no one thought that the least bit odd or irresponsible. On one occasion I happened to be one of the last two to leave the lounge having had coffee. I walked out of the hotel nattering to my friend, who as it happened, was one of the group that did not have a child. We walked along the road for a bit and when our ways parted, she waved cheerio to me, and I carried on a little bit further to my house. When I was about to put the key in the lock of the door, I suddenly realised that I wasn't carrying very much — where was all the shopping? I instantly remembered where the shopping was — it was in the pram and indeed so was my baby — and where was the pram? — still outside the door of the Royal Hotel! I turned on my heel and tried to not to look panic-stricken, nor to run, as I made my way back, as fast as (whilst maintaining some dignity) I possibly could, to discover that the pram was still there and the shopping was still there and, thank goodness, the baby was still there. The latter cooing and waving his legs and feet in the air and generally smiling at anybody who bothered to glance at him. I gathered up the pram with its precious contents and, trying to stop my heart from beating so hard that it felt as though it going to come out of my chest, I walked quietly home. It was a long while before I admitted that incident to anyone.

I think I already mentioned that there were lots of social events that went on in Thurso, often at HMS Vulcan. Now that sounds as though it ought to be a ship. In fact, it was not, it was a building on dry land, but it was a Royal Naval establishment and, apparently, it is traditional to give Royal Naval establishments the name of a ship and the chap in charge is usually referred to as the captain or the commander. These social events were put on to entertain the Naval community, but also included local people, the atomic families and men from an American air force base that was also in Thurso. The theme of one event was the 'Wild West' and we were all to go in fancy dress. It so happened that this event was the very weekend that my mother decided to come to visit. We couldn't put her off; we didn't *want* to put her off. Once she was with us, we couldn't leave her at home; we didn't *want* to leave her at home, so she had to have a Wild West fancy dress and, not surprisingly, she hadn't brought one with her. Now the town wasn't the sort to have a shopping centre or department stores, so I had a very serious think as to what I could do to create a wearable fancy dress for my mum at somewhat short notice.

As it happened, I still had a dark green straight tunic which I had made as a maternity dress and what I thought was, if I could buy some colourful braids and some fringing, I could put them on the said tunic and, with a suitable headdress and feather, I could make my mother a reasonably good costume as a Native American squaw. Where might I get the braid and the fringing? The answer was Miss Miller-Calder's shop.

Miss Miller-Calder's shop was technically a furniture shop; it consisted of a very small foyer in which there was nothing but a fairly rough-hewn bench with a till and then big double doors that opened into a huge warehouse. In the warehouse, there was every sort of furniture you could possibly imagine from cheap tat to valuable antiques, from Formica to Chippendale. The day I chose to go to buy, if possible, the said fringing, it was pouring with rain. I had small child in a pram, I had an umbrella, I had a plastic mac. I got myself and my clutter into the little foyer of Miss Miller-Calder's shop. I could see her standing just inside the big double doors of the warehouse talking to another lady who was wearing a smart gaberdine raincoat with a silk scarf tied around her head. They didn't seem to notice that I and my son were there, and we dripped. The pram dripped, the umbrella dripped, my plastic mac dripped, and we were making quite a puddle on the floor. After a little while, I thought I've got to do something, so I said "Excuse me, ladies. I'm sorry to interrupt your conversation but are you able to help me?"

They turned around, smiled at me, and one of them said, "Oh, I do apologise, we didn't realise you were there."

It was the Queen Mother, my second encounter with that lady, visiting her Scottish home, the castle of Mey, and apparently catching up with a long-standing friend — I was told that she and Miss Miller-Calder had been 'gels' together. I am pleased to report that the two ladies, when I explained what I wanted, were very helpful. They provided excellent service; the Queen Mother took as much interest in selecting braid and fringing for my mother's fancy dress costume as any shop assistant could and I went away a very satisfied customer. There ought to be a third encounter and there was. My small son had never seen trees; Thurso does have trees but none of them are tall. When we went south for his christening, he loved being in the garden under these mystical things that waved, moved and looked pretty. When we went back to Thurso someone said to me the only place up here where you will find tall luscious deciduous trees is in the garden of the Castle of Mey. I'm pleased to say we were allowed to visit, so it was, indirectly, the Queen Mother who provided my son with another one of his very early experiences, which like everything else, he seemed to enjoy hugely. I'll talk to you again soon. Bye-bye.

6. Retail Experience

By the time my son was six months old, the roller-coaster life that I had lived since I got married, moved to Thurso, had a baby and two different jobs, seemed to be calming down. I was in a very comfortable position, with a lovely baby, lots of friends, plenty to do and enjoy and a pattern to my life which enabled me, finally, to pass my driving test. At some point in this period, we moved in to one of the brand-new houses that the Atomic Energy Authority provided for their employees. The departure from our little rented house was not without incident. We obviously wanted to leave our affairs in order; we'd sorted out the rent, no problem; we'd paid the electricity bill, no problem, and then I went to the Gas Board to pay the gas bill. Here, I was met by a terribly efficient, perhaps even officious, assistant who was adamant that they did not provide gas to number 10, Sinclair Street. I *lived* in number 10, Sinclair Street; I'd had a new baby whilst living there; we had cooked on a gas stove, washed our clothes in a gas boiler; washed ourselves with water heated by the gas water heater, not to mention using the very strange drying device that I described to you before. But it was no good arguing with the young woman, because she did not have a card in her filing system for the house I was talking about, therefore, they did not provide gas to that house, therefore, I had no bill to pay. I didn't argue. I gave her my forwarding address and since all of this happened pretty nearly sixty years ago, I don't imagine that anyone is ever going to decide that it was a mistake. I can only assume that the bills were being delivered to the part of the building that had long since been closed off and to which we had no access - since it fronted a different road it may well have had a different address.

So, life was on even keel, but things were not going to stay like that for very long. Why? Because I went back to work. I didn't seek to go back to work, you understand, I wasn't looking for a job and the question of maternity leave from my teaching post didn't arise in the years that I'm talking about. One evening I went with my husband and a group of our friends to one of the socials that from time to occurred at the Naval Base and during the course of the evening, I happened to dance with the local jeweller, who was called John. His wife and my husband and got to know each other through playing in the town badminton club. John was saying that he was not looking forward to Monday — this was Saturday evening. Why not? Because his shop assistant had very recently resigned and left. She and her husband were moving south as he was going to a different job and, that very day, John's apprentice had gone into hospital with appendicitis. This meant that, on Monday, John would have the shop all to himself, no shop assistant, no apprentice, and he didn't know how he would manage. I commented, just casually, "Oh well, if I didn't have a small baby to look after, I would be pleased come and rescue you, if you would have me."

I thought no more of it until the next day, Sunday, when we had a visit from John and his wife, Vi. They had come to say that they would like to take up my offer of helping in the jewellery shop in the emergency and that Vi had agreed — I hope she agreed happily — that she would look after my son, because she already had two small children and, in her own words, "To add an extra one when you've already got two really isn't going to be a problem". Furthermore, since they lived above the shop, I would always be to hand if needed. Well, if that's what she believed, good for her. So, it was decided that I would for a short while 'in the emergency' go each day to the jeweller's shop for one o'clock so that John could have some lunch and then I would continue to work there until about half past five or six o'clock when the shop closed. The scheme worked — it worked rather well, because 'the emergency' lasted for two years!

I continued to work at John's shop until I left Thurso. I had ventured into the retail business twice before; on neither occasion did I want to do the job permanently. For a short while, in one of my university holidays, I had worked in a greengrocer's on the main shopping street in Maidstone, the High Street. The shop had an open front and a roller shutter that was pushed up in the mornings and came right down at night, so the shop was like a market stall, but right in the middle of a busy high road. One Saturday afternoon when things got a bit frantic with people, traffic, dust and din, I realised that I wasn't entirely coping when I called out to a friend, as I put eggs into the big pan on the weighing machine, "How much are eggs a pound?" I was teased unmercifully for that thereafter and decided that greengrocery and I — even though greengrocery doesn't normally include eggs — were not a good combination.

The other job that I had was in Boyd's Electrical — if you could plug it in, or switch it on, they sold it. I worked there for several weeks in the period between leaving university and starting my first teaching post. If I'd had any intention of going into the retail business, I would have been off to a good start, as when I had been at Boyd's for just a fortnight, I was made assistant manager. Any ambitions that I might have had, and I didn't have any, of staying in that trade completely vanished out of the window because of background music. In those days one could try out a record in a booth at the shop before buying it. Please note, the booths were not soundproof and several weeks of 'Johnny Remember Me', over and over, and over and over again, made it quite clear to me that I didn't want to work anywhere near recorded music.

I envisaged that working in a jewellery shop would be calm and elegant and for a lot of the time it was. Sometimes, especially in the mornings, it was almost too calm. Besides selling things, the shop did lots of watch and clock repairs so, when it was calm, my job was to prepare and send out accounts. That wasn't the easiest job in the world, not because of my mathematics, but because conversations like this occurred. I would say, "John, you haven't given me any information about how much Miss Somebody's repair is going to cost for her watch," and John would say, "Oh she's the midwife, you can't charge her for her watch, she needs it."

On one occasion, I said, "John, I haven't had any invoice information for Mr and Mrs So-and-so for their clock repair."

And in reply he said, "Ah, they gave me a sack of potatoes last year before the winter."

Then the most mysterious one of all. Opposite the jewellery shop was the big Hydro Electricity Board showroom, and in the window, there were a couple of magnificent chest freezers. Every year, one of John's jobs would be to service all the clocks in the showroom — that would include the time clocks which switched the lighting in the windows on and off, so that they were illuminated after dark when the shop was closed. I had never seen a bill for these services and when trying to prepare one, I discovered that John's hobby in life — when he wasn't being a jeweller — was that he was a very successful trout and salmon fisherman. And where did his catch get stored? In the said chest freezers in the Hydro Electricity Board shop window.

Near Christmas however, working in the shop was just frantic and I particularly remember one afternoon when I put a kettle on to boil on the gas ring in the little back office, so that I could make a cup of tea for us to have when things quietened down. Things didn't quieten down; there was customer after customer, after customer, all buying Christmas present-y things and suddenly there was the most dreadful smell. I went out to see what was happening and found that all the water in the little kettle had boiled dry and when I went to attempt to take the kettle off the stove, the bottom fell out of it completely. I must have been well regarded by my boss because he decided, after I had been working in the shop for some while, that he and Vi would take a holiday. They would go away for a week and leave me in charge. I was very proud of this responsibility and assured them that all would be well.

Having made alternative child-care arrangements for the week, I went into work on Monday morning, and all was fine for about half an hour. James the apprentice, the one who had been in hospital with appendicitis, was long since fully recovered and was working in the back workroom. After the shop had been open for the said half an hour, he came bursting into the showroom, where all the sales occurred, saying "Jeanie, Jeanie, the shop's on fire! The shop's on fire!" I can still hear myself answering in my best 'English' voice, "Oh, James, don't exaggerate!"

I went into the workroom and indeed that room and the back office were full of black smoke. Thankfully, there was, of course, no one in the flat upstairs, which is where the family and my son would normally have been, so we shut the door to the stairs so that the smoke didn't go up to the flat above. I sent James out to the front door of the shop with instructions to make sure that he didn't let any customers come in and I managed to find my way through the smoke to the little office where the phone was, to ring for the fire brigade. The fire brigade came remarkably quickly which is surprising because, in a town like Thurso, most of the firemen were volunteers and they had to drop whatever they were doing in their normal day job in order to come and gather together as the fire squad. I sometimes wondered what would happen if the firemen and the lifeboat men were required at one at the same time because I was pretty sure they were pretty much the same stalwart men.

The biggest decision that I had to make about that fire was whether to tell Vi and John what had happened before they came back at the end of the week. Fortunately, I decided not to tell them. You will understand, this was years before we all had mobile phones and contacting them wasn't going to be easy. When they came back I was able to reassure them that no damage had been done to the structure of the building and that most of the mess caused by the smoke and water had been dealt with. To this day, I am sure that James was probably smoking whilst cleaning watch parts in a tray of cleaning fluid. He always insisted that he was not, and no one could ever really find out. The biggest problem was insurance; everything the shop owned was insured straightforwardly, but all customers' goods in for repair had to be sorted out between, those insured by the shop, if there was no other insurance, and those insured by the owners if they had their own insurance. It took forever, but we did have a very smart newly painted shop at the end of it all. I forgave James; John forgave me, and he even thanked me for not telling him of the fire until the end of his family holiday. Working in a jeweller's shop was a good experience for me; I got to see a different side of the town that, for a while, was my home. The best thing of all was that my little boy grew up, not as an only child, but with the rough and tumble of two surrogate sibling sisters! Bye-bye.

7. Odds and Sods

Good evening. Lerner and Loewe's musical *Brigadoon* is set in the Highlands of Scotland and in that show, there is a wedding. The wedding scene begins with the clans gathering for the ceremony. They come in, one clan at a time, take up their positions and proudly call out the name of their clan. I had the female lead in that show, a long time ago; a character called Fiona, and I well remember a rehearsal which caused a great deal of laughter. Usually, in the middle of a rehearsal, there was a tea break, and everybody would have a cup of tea or coffee, but in the case of the rehearsals for *Brigadoon*, we were rehearsing somewhere where there was a hostelry just across the road and it was not unusual for a group of the younger persons, mostly men, in the company to go across for 'a wee dram' when it was the tea break. On this occasion, after the tea break, we were going to rehearse the wedding scene, so the clans, somewhat depleted, arrived and called out their names: Campbell, McDonald, Sinclair, McGregor. All the people in the room had arrived and we hadn't actually got to the end of music. At that moment the door to the room burst open and in came the stragglers who had been having their refreshments across in the pub. They marched forward and one of them called out in a loud and cheerful voice, "Odds and Sods."

The rehearsal fell about in laughter, apart from the director, who was somewhat irritable at the best of times Perhaps it would be fair to mention here, that the production was taking place in England. All of the performers were English, but the director wasn't… his name was Jock.

There wasn't a Musical Society of the sort that did operas or operettas in Thurso when I lived there, but there was plenty of opportunity to sing and mostly the singing took place in the local Choral Union, which I'm pleased to say still exists and flourishes. Once a year there would be the big Choral Union event and we sang some very notable works. I remember *The Messiah, The Creation, Hiawatha's Wedding Feast* and *The Christmas Oratorio,* and I particularly remember the occasion when we did one of Mozart's major works. Now, you have to know, that we used to rehearse in the high school, but we used to perform the big concerts in the Church of Scotland. Preparations normally went smoothly, and we usually got a good audience. On this particular year, rehearsals were going all right, we were getting near to the date of the show and posters started to go up around the town, in order for us to start selling the tickets, and what were we going to sing? Mozart's *Requiem.* It was at this point, that one of the church elders saw a poster and said, "Och, ye cannae do a Papist Mass in the Church of Scotland."

The fact that some of the members of the Church of Scotland were singing in the Choral Union and the fact that a good many of the church members would normally buy tickets to come, wasn't the issue. There was no argument about the merit of the work; the problem was the poster, it could not be seen to announce that the Church of Scotland was going to have a Requiem, a Papist Mass. The matter was fairly quickly resolved, because the church authorities allowed us to have our deposit back and we moved the performance, fairly smoothly, to the main hall of the high school where we rehearsed. By the next year, it was all back to normal again. The lesson we had to learn was, that it's not what you do, it's what you say you're going to do on the poster, that matters.

A group of us who liked to sing more informally, would rehearse sometimes in a very strange venue, the venue was somebody's greenhouse, because that was the only place big enough in their home for the piano. One year, the thing that three of us rehearsed was, *Three Little Maids from School* from *The Mikado* and we entered the Thurso Musical Festival Ladies Over 16 Ensemble Class. When we got to the event, we discovered that there were three other girls singing the same song in the same class and they were senior pupils from the high school, so they would have been perhaps

191

sixteen or seventeen. We were much older, early twenties. When the Class was finished and the adjudicator got up to announce the winners, we three ladies were delighted when she said, "The Maturer Maids have it!"

I was one of the Maturer Maids. It was only then, that we discovered that, because we'd won our Class, we were invited to sing in the End of Festival Winners Concert. On the appointed evening, we all turned up at the Town Hall — three of us and our male pianist — to perform in the concert. When we saw the programme, we discovered that we were item 28. It was going to be a long time before item 28 was performing, so we went across to the nearest hostelry to 'have a wee dram' and then went back to the Town Hall to see how things were going, only to discover that it was still a long way away from item 28. So, we went back to the hostelry again, had 'another wee dram' and, when we got back this time, it was pretty much time for us to perform. Our male pianist produced from his bag a large flask of black coffee and we all had a drink of that before we went on to do our bit. I think our bit went very well; there was much applause and we all felt that we'd done a good job. It was only after we all got home again that the wife of our pianist said, "How did it go?" and we said we thought it went fine and she said, "Well, when I made you the flask of coffee, I thought you might be nervous and so I put a large slug of whiskey in it. Well, it did go well! My memory of the details is, not surprisingly, a bit faint.

Being in Thurso could be dangerous. Working at the Atomic Energy Authority could be dangerous, and everyone wore film badges to indicate how much exposure to radioactivity they had encountered. The site technicians spent a long time working out how much time the scientists could stay in various areas of the site. It was a standing joke, among the scientists, that the technicians would take twenty-three minutes, with their sophisticated equipment, in order to be able to tell the scientists that they had seven minutes and fourteen seconds safe working time. Another part of Thurso that could be dangerous, and more immediately so, was the sea. My husband used to say that if he came out of his office on a very gusty day, when the wind was powerful, he was in danger of being swept off the mainland and out across the sea. All the while he was on the mainland, because of the situation of his office, he could legitimately say he was the top scientist in Britain. The place to go, if you wanted the sea and some peace, was not Thurso beach. Thurso did have a beach, but that was usually very busy and if you got up early enough in the morning, you could buy fish and shellfish from the boats as they came in with their catches. If you wanted quiet and natural beauty, you went to Dunnet Head, where the sand dunes were. It was very windy at Dunnet Head, but because of the sand dunes you could always find a cosy place where the wind would whistle over the top of you and the dunes would shelter you and keep you warm. I was never very good at sunbathing and one day, when as a family, we were out at the dunes, while my husband and son, who went brown easily, were sunning themselves, I took myself for a walk along the shore. Suddenly, I found myself part of Hitchcock's film, *The Birds*. If you've ever been dive-bombed by birds, you will know it is very scary and I was dive-bombed by lots of birds. The birds in question were Arctic terns, quite big birds with very sharp, hooked bills. I didn't know why I was so attractive to them, and I wished I wasn't. In order to get away, I ran up the beach nearer to the sand dunes, only to realise when I'd only gone about a metre or so up from where I had been walking, that the birds turned away and ignored me completely. So, danger notwithstanding, I walked back down to the path I had been walking along and, lo and behold, the flotilla of birds reappeared instantly. I discovered afterwards that the Arctic terns lay their eggs along the high-water line, and I had been walking along the high-water line. The moment I was away from their eggs, they completely lost interest in me.

All too soon, our time in Thurso was coming to an end, it was time to move on. Time to get out of the shelter of the dunes and venture forth into the big world. I had arrived in Thurso in fear and trepidation as to what I might find. What did I find? I found a welcome; I found friendship. I found friendship that lasted. There are still people that we made friends with sixty years ago that we're in touch with now. I acquired a baby, a son, and I'm now a grandmother. Ironically, I am now married to someone called Gemmell, whose antecedents are Scottish. Gemmell is a Scottish name, it means 'the old one', so it gets more appropriate as the years go by. But perhaps the most important thing that I found in Thurso was myself.

I hope you've enjoyed listening to these recollections of a period of my life that was a long time ago. The stories are as accurate as I can make them, within my memory. Thank you very much. It's lovely talking to you. Bye-bye

'Tis the Season to be Jolly

1. Deck the Hall

Hello everyone. It's the 1st of December 2020. This morning I was woken up to Classic FM on my bedside table radio playing Christmas carols. That prompted me to decide that now is the time to talk to you again and to share some reminiscences of Christmases past in my life and, as usual, they are stories that I hope you will find funny and amusing. Before I embark on that though, I want to share with you that I'm very fond of crossword puzzles and the like, as one of the ways to keep myself entertained. I would recommend to you, if you want a puzzle that's a bit difficult to resolve, look at the government instructions for three households meeting, over what is now not the twelve, but the five days of Christmas. I had a long phone conversation with a friend last night about our differing interpretations of those instructions and we decided we would go away to read them again and get back to each other this morning. When I did go away and read them again, I thought her interpretation was right and mine was wrong, so imagine my surprise when, shortly after I woke up this morning, the phone rang, and it was my friend. She said that having read the instructions again, her interpretation was wrong and mine was right! That cannot be, can it? I can't offer a prize for the first satisfactory solution, but I do hope someone's going to clarify the rules before we get to the point of having to implement them.

About this time last year, or it may have been the year before, I was invited to give a talk to entertain the ladies of a Morning Coffee Club at the end of their Christmas lunch party. The secretary asked me to deliver a talk which was related to Christmas. I hadn't such a talk ready, so I put together lots of snippets, bits and bobs that were Christmassy stories of experiences I had had, and remembered, and I called the whole thing, "Deck The Hall". When I arrived at the venue, somewhere I'd never been before, I was welcomed by the secretary and shown in. The room was long and thin, with the door at one of the narrow ends and the top table where the committee of the group had been having their lunch at the far end. The room was warm and festive, very well decorated and my welcome was also warm. The decorations were enhanced by the fact that the ladies had decided on a dress code for the occasion, which involved all of them wearing Christmas sweaters. So, there were robins and reindeer, sleighs and stars, Christmas trees, Christmas crackers, Christmas puddings… in fact, all of the symbols of the Season. It looked very jolly indeed. Down at the far end, near the top table, a number of ladies were standing talking and one of them, it transpired, was the Lady President or Chairman of the group; I'm not sure which she was called. Someone pointed out to her that the guest speaker had arrived, and she turned round to come to welcome me. She was a big woman, not fat, but statuesque I think would be the word. She was also an enthusiastic woman and she bounced merrily down the room to greet me, her guest. I use the word 'bounced' advisedly, she was endowed with extraordinarily large breasts; a bosom that could be described as 'magnificent' and the breasts, besides being impressive in size, appeared to be independent in suspension, because, as she came down the room, they bounced and jostled in a very jolly manner. I now have to tell you that her chosen Christmas jumper was emblazoned with a large bunch of brightly coloured satin balloons and that the two very biggest balloons could not possibly have been more strategically placed! I hoped, and sent up a silent prayer to the effect, that my face muscles were under total control.

Now my name is Jean Gemmell; if I want to be grand, I'm Jean Gemmell, Lady of the Manor of Fenton, and I was at the lunch because I was going to give a talk called, 'Deck the Hall'.

She introduced me enthusiastically to her members saying, "We're delighted to be able to listen today to Jean Fenton, who's going to talk to us about Interior Decorating."

Well, I delivered the talk that I had planned to deliver, and nobody seemed to notice that it didn't relate to the title that had been announced. I'm pleased to say we all had a splendid time, including me, and the warmth of, dare I call her this, 'The Balloon Lady' could not be over emphasised.

Now why did I call my Christmas talk, 'Deck the Hall'? It was because, years and years ago, I used that title for a concert I remember vividly, which I put together at Derby Guildhall. I'd been commissioned to do it by Radio Derby and the plan was that the concert would be performed to a live audience. The performance would be recorded, then on Christmas morning, it would go out on air. I had chosen as the format for the concert a selection of well-known and well-loved books that had stories relating to Christmas in them. I particularly remember that I used Fezziwig's Party from *A Christmas Carol* and I used the extract in *Little Women*, where the March Girls go to deliver gifts to some of the people that were suffering hardship in their village on that Christmas morning. Then the bit where Moley gets very unhappy and homesick for his little home when he's out with Ratty, which is in *Wind in the Willows* or *Toad of Toad Hall*, depending on whether you're familiar with the book or the play. Dressed in a posh frock, sitting in a splendid leather armchair at the front corner of the stage, I introduced each little story snippet. To the side of me was a small table, on which stood a pile of beautifully bound leather books: I have to admit they were chosen for their attractive appearance and their content bore no resemblance to that purported to be in them. Every little scene was dramatized and included a song or a piece of orchestral music.

The show got off to a good start and was going 'great guns', until we arrived at an excerpt that had been dramatized in *Oh What A Lovely War*. The occasion described was when, in the First World War, on Christmas night, hostilities ceased and the Tommies in the trenches were thrown gifts of chocolate and tobacco by the German soldiers. At that time, I gather, men from each warring army even came out of the trenches and played football in No Man's Land. I had staged the scene so that the British contingent, which included my husband, was in full view of the audience in a dugout that was made of sandbags and the German contingent was in the wings. The 'British' soldiers had to learn their dialogue, but the 'German' soldiers had their copy of the play in front of them. The idea was that there should be an exchange of greetings and song between the two opposing armies and then a jackboot containing gifts would be thrown in and the whole item would end with the men getting out of the trenches and singing 'Silent Night' in German and in English.

This scene had gone quite well at the rehearsal, but when it came to the actual performance, I am afraid things became chaotic when one of the actors playing a German soldier, unseen of course by the audience, managed to turn over two pages in his script at once and thought it was the moment for throwing in the boot — which he promptly did. The boot was large and landed with a thud, and miles too soon. The scene was nowhere near the end; dialogue had been cut; the singing hadn't happened and the 'British Tommies', in my hearing, made comments which were most certainly not in the script. I was sitting quite near to the wings of the stage and managed to stage-whisper and gesticulate to the chap in charge of the curtain to close it as quickly as possible and bring the scene to an abrupt end, which he did. After the show, when I met with the 'German' team, I was pretty cross but, never mind, the rest of the evening had gone smoothly.

On Christmas morning my family had gone out in the car to deliver some presents and on our way back home, we were driving through a village near where I lived and saw one of the erstwhile pretend German soldiers, who was out walking his dog. I wound down the car window, as we stopped, to exchange greetings. His greeting to me was, "I don't know what you were on about after that performance the other night. I listened to the broadcast this morning and there wasn't anything wrong with it at all."

Well, no, of course there wasn't, because the producer, one of the technicians at Radio Derby, and I had taken what seemed like a whole morning — probably three quarters of an hour — to edit the shambles of that scene and put it back together, so that it was as it was meant to be. Fortunately, some of the rehearsal had been recorded, so bits of the rehearsal could be cut and pasted in to where the devastation was worst. At the time that I am remembering, 'cut and paste' didn't mean something you did on a computer, it meant, literally slicing through bits of recording tape and sticking them back together again. *C'est la vie,* the excerpt was rescued and went out on air sounding quite splendid. Everybody sang 'Silent Night' with gusto — I'm not sure you're meant to sing 'Silent Night' with gusto — but that's how I remember it. That concert was entitled 'Deck the Hall', not 'Interior Decorating'. I look forward to talking to you again very soon. I hope my ramblings bring a smile to your face and encourage you to remember some of your past Christmases which, perhaps not at the time, but seen in retrospect, were funny. Bye-bye.

2. Christmas Lights

Hello! Good evening. My father was a baker; more specifically, he was a pastry confectioner. He specialised in icing cakes and making beautiful gateaux, so at Christmas time, his life was rather busy. At home, however, it was always my mother who did the cooking, (except on very rare, very special occasions) and her cooking was good, including her Christmas cakes, rich fruit cake, plenty of brandy, lashings of marzipan — I'm very fond of marzipan — and lots of royal icing. My mother had two favourite designs for her Christmas cakes, and they tended to be indicative of the way her preparations for Christmas were going. If she was feeling fraught and all the jobs were getting a bit much, the Christmas cake design would be a snow scene. You've probably done a snow scene, nearly everyone has, they're nice and easy. You put a lot of royal icing on the top of the marzipan and then you flick up the icing with a fork. Then you have some little commercially bought novelty figures, these days plastic, in my youth probably plaster of Paris, that you dot around on the top — little reindeer, or a snowman, or robins, or something like that. You cover the sides of the cake by buying or making a paper frill, they look pretty, and for all its simplicity the cake tastes fine. If my mother's preparations for Christmas were going smoothly and she was feeling calm about things, then we would have a more formal design on the top of the cake, one that was piped, and usually it would be a star. My mother's stars always emphasised the Jewish nature of the event, not because my mother wished to stress the fact that the Christ Child was a Jew but because the Star of David, which has six points, is a lot easier to draw than the Bethlehem Star which has five points. Most people can manage a six-pointed star, but a five-pointed star is a lot trickier. That leads me on to my first story about Christmas lights. No! I don't mean the tangle of wire and LEDs that were working fine when you took them off the tree one year and never seem to want to work at all when you go to put them on the tree the next year. The particular light that I'm talking about on this occasion was a Star of Bethlehem. I would have been about seven and my dancing school always did a Christmas concert. This was the first year that I had a solo spot in the Christmas concert, and I wanted it to be very splendid. I was very proud; I was going to sing a song called 'The Old Lamp Lighter of Long, Long Ago'. I'm sorry to admit I can't remember anything about the words of the song and I've not the faintest idea what the tune was like, but I do remember the title and I do remember my outfit. Little green dungarees, a Wee

Willy Winky pom-pom hat and I had a lantern to carry, the lantern attached to a pole. All of the costume was made, apart from one vital part of the design that my dancing schoolteacher required: that the bib of my dungarees should have emblazoned upon it a five-pointed Star of Bethlehem in gold-coloured sequins. Now my mum, as I've just said, was only ever any good at doing the Star of David with six points. My dad, who was very good at the Star of Bethlehem, or any other sort of star for that matter, was unfortunately ill. During the Second World War he'd been stationed in French North Africa and while he was there, he'd contracted something called sandfly fever. It's not unlike malaria but not nearly, I think, so serious, but it does tend to recur in bouts, from time to time for a long while after you've actually recovered from the first attack. My father was having one of his bouts of sandfly fever and the date of the concert was getting nearer and nearer. My mother had tried drawing some five-pointed stars on tracing paper before putting anything onto the costume, but they'd not been very successful, so she threw sympathy to the winds and nagged my poor dad to wake up, get up, design and put onto my dungarees the vital five-pointed star, which with a little bit of grumbling, he did. Then, having got involved, he decided, since he'd drawn the star onto the dungarees, he'd put all the sequins on as well and by the time he'd finished that, he decided, rather surprisingly, that he'd recovered. I went to thank him for my five-pointed star, I was very much a daddy's girl, and I thanked him for doing a lovely star on my costume, "Especially, when you were so very poorly."

And he said bravely, "Oh don't worry darling! I wasn't as poorly as all that, it was only sandfly fever." I said, "Oh no it wasn't."

"What do you mean?" he said.

I replied, "I told Nana and Nana said, you didn't have sandfly fever, you had something much worse." "What did I have that was much worse?" he asked.

I replied solemnly, "You had Idle-itis." I don't know what happened after that... I didn't know that 'Idle-itis' was a made-up word, to do with wanting to say snug in bed on a cold day. Never mind, I had my costume. I haven't got a picture of me in that costume. I've got a picture of me rehearsing for the show in my dancing school rehearsal outfit plus my lantern, so I know that it happened, but the star that shone so brightly has unfortunately vanished over the years, but it does lead me tidily on to my next story.

My next story concerns the only time that I was ever in a pantomime. Now, as already mentioned, the all-girls school that I attended in my secondary school years gave me plenty of opportunity to dance and to sing and to be in public performances and plays, but I always seemed to be cast as a boy and I did want to be cast on at least one occasion as a girl. This, however, was not the occasion, because, in this production, I actually wanted to be the boy. There's something very splendid about being the Principal Boy in a pantomime but was I the Principal Boy? Oh no! I was not. This time I did have a female role: I was cast as the Wicked Witch. The pantomime in question was called *The Tinderbox Man*, not one of the front runners in the pantomime league table but the wicked witch did have one big important scene. For some reason, which has long since escaped me, she had to make a spell and the spell was about the moon rising, and the rays of the moon falling on a gnarled old tree, where carved into the bark of the tree was the secret sign or symbol which led one to the treasure. I had the spell, and the spell was all rhyming couplets. When it came to my scene, there I was, with my pointed hat and my crooked nose and my haggardly fingernails, and I did my little spell for the moon to rise and light on the tree. Unfortunately, I was only just into the spell when I realised the spell was not going to be very effective; the moon was not going to rise. Why not? Because the moon was created by the light from a follow-spot on the balcony at the back of our school hall and the lighting operator of the said follow-spot was my best mate, Jennifer, who was sitting, thoroughly enjoying the pantomime in the front row of the audience. She didn't have many lighting cues and she had decided that until it was her moment, she would sit and enjoy the show. Well, that's fair enough, except when it *was* her moment, she was still enjoying the show. I made up couplet after couplet:

"Oh dear moon light,
Please shine so bright,

For if you don't,
I'm in a plight."

They were the sort of couplets that I made up as I went along, and I glared at her and hoped that by some power of mind I would actually get through to her that there was a crisis. That worked, except that when it did work, it didn't happen subtly. She suddenly shrieked, "Oh!", jumped to her feet and pounded across in front of the front row, out of the door at the front of the hall, down the corridor at the side of the hall and up the stairs at the back of the hall. She had on good sensible shoes, on our school's good parquet floor, and so every single footfall was audible to everyone in the audience. She arrived at the follow-spot, which of course wasn't switched on, whilst I was still ad-libbing the longest spell ever. Now, if you've ever operated a follow-spot, which you probably haven't, you will know that before you switch it on, you have to make sure that the aperture is very small and you also have to make sure that there is a gauze filter across the aperture so that when the light comes on, it is only small in size, dim and hazy. Then, when you know it's pointed in the right place you open the aperture, and you bring up the intensity of the light. Well, that's what should happen, but in her panic my friend Jennifer just flicked the switch to on and the light shone forth in full blaze, on completely the wrong place on the stage. So, she frantically whizzed it round and it looked for all the world like a searchlight that circled the night sky in the Second World War when the ack-ack gunners were trying to pick up enemy planes to shoot them down. It wasn't subtle at all. Eventually, the light fell upon the exotic symbol carved on the tree and, when it did, there was tremendous applause, but for her, the technician, not for the aspiring poet, me! Oh dear! Of course, the spell worked because the rest of the pantomime wouldn't have carried on otherwise. Christmas Lights, they've always been a problem. I'll tell you another Christmas story on another day. Bye-bye.

3. Santa Stories

Rudolph with your nose so bright,
Won't you guide our sleigh tonight?

Well good evening. For Rudolph, read me. Nose so bright? Well, I hope not; consider a torch or a flashlight. Sleigh? My father's trusty Morris Minor. One foggy Christmas Eve? Absolutely, definitely.

Now, in our family, throughout the years of my childhood and my youth, my aunty Kath had a television and a telephone, my grandmother had a grand piano, my nan had a parrot, and my dad had a car. So, it was usually the case that, on Christmas Eve, it would be my dad, my brother, my mother and I who did the Christmas present run. This involved us taking our Christmas presents to some other person's house and then collecting some, perhaps for us and then collecting some to take to another house, and so on and so forth. We'd done it several times and so we knew what we were about. On this particular year, in the afternoon, my younger brother's friend, Tony, had been at our house playing and he opened the door and looked out and he called out to me as I was nearby, "Jean, the fog ain't 'alf fick."

So, I said to him, "Tony, it's not 'F', it's, 'Th'…" He nodded sagely. Later on, when he thought it was time for him to go home so that we could set out on our little voyage, he opened the door and he said, "Jean the thog ain't 'alf fick."

I don't think he ever did sort out 'F' and 'Th', but his observation was right, the fog was very thick. Nonetheless, we intrepid travellers set off with our presents and for probably two-thirds of the afternoon and evening all was well, until we were making our way back home again and then the fog was 'a pea-souper'. I don't think, these days, we get fog that is as bad as that smog was, since the Clean Air Act and all that sort of thing. I had to get out of the car, find the flashlight in the door pocket, discover happily that it worked, and I had to walk ahead of the car, shining the flashlight onto the curb, so that my father could slowly drive behind me and we could find our way back home. So, I know exactly how Rudolph must have felt, but we succeeded, and our journey and our deliveries were all successfully concluded.

Remembering things that happened at Christmas is very good fun. I'll tell you another story. For some years I was deputy head of a big comprehensive school on the boundary between Derbyshire and Nottinghamshire. It was a very well-appointed school and among other things it boasted a purpose-built sixth form suite, which was an L-shaped, carpeted, multi-purpose first floor room. It could be used as a lounge area, for lectures or for films and off this area there was a terrace, a balcony built on the roof of the craft room that was below. It looked very attractive with wooden planters with shrubs and flowers which the school gardener kept in good order. Unfortunately, the pupils never used it, nor, for that matter, the staff, because it was dangerous. There was, would you believe, no handrail round this terrace, just a parapet at about a suitable height for sitting on, fifteen inches or so high, and that was it. Health and Safety, it would seem, had not been a priority for the architect who had designed it aiming for an attractive, sophisticated appearance. In those days, schools did not run their own budgets for buildings and maintenance and although every year we asked for a substantial handrail to be put around the said terrace, it came very low in the batting order of things that were to be done.

One of my jobs was overseeing the termly Governors Health and Safety Inspection and one particular winter term, we hadn't got around to it until it was nearly time to break up for the Christmas holidays. So, after school, one night, I was showing the group of governors that formed the Health and Safety committee around the school. All had gone swimmingly; no one had raised any particular issues and we were nearing the end of our trip. We were up in the sixth-form suite and, since I've got quite good eyesight — at least I did have then, I noticed to my dismay that the door onto the terrace was not locked. It wasn't even closed. It was standing ajar, and the key was in the lock. I was actually very grateful when, at that point, the governors' attention was attracted by the noise of happy laughter and singing from the voices of some very young children and, while they were moving forward around the L-shape of the area to see what the attractive noises were, I quietly shut the door, turned the key and put it in my pocket. When I caught up with the governors, we were in the middle of a very happy, jolly, little party. Some of the pupils at the school were doing NVQs rather than GCSEs and as part of the NVQ in Child Care they had mounted a Christmas party for the children that they had used as their case studies during their term of working with young people. They had lots of nice things to eat, they had party games and the school music teacher was there playing tunes and everyone was singing and there was some dancing. One little child told me, they were having a lovely time and looking forward to Santa coming. The governors and I moved on, finished our Health and Safety visit and that was that. Well, it was until the next morning, when I went into school. I happened to see the teacher who'd been in charge of the course, and I said, "You seemed to be having a very successful party with your young people last night," and she said to me, "We were, until the children sang 'Rudolph the Red-nosed Reindeer', which was the signal for Santa Claus to arrive. He didn't arrive; he *couldn't* arrive; he was out on the balcony and couldn't get back in because somebody had locked the door and had taken away the key. The caretaker couldn't find the spare key and when he finally did, it was raining, so Santa was sopping wet when he eventually arrived at the party, and it was a wonder all the presents weren't sopping wet as well."

I tried to keep a straight face and simply said, "Oh dear!"

I don't think I ever owned up to many people that I had been the person that had stopped Santa coming.

There was another occasion when I didn't stop Santa coming. We had an event at Kilburn Hall when two different Women's Institutes gathered together for a Christmas meal. The two secretaries that had organised the event on behalf of their groups were very different in style. One was laid back, happy about most things and not given to bothering too much about detail, the other was punctilious and believed in lists and times, etc. so when people arrived, one group knew exactly what the seating plan was, and the other group had no idea and didn't care. When it came to getting their main courses, one group had little cards on which were written what they had ordered and the other group didn't know, couldn't't remember and didn't mind much, and so it had gone on all evening. When I'd asked if anyone was going to say grace, both of the secretaries sprang to their feet and then, one of them looked grumpy and the other one laughed, and I think I said grace, because that way there wasn't any aggravation. They were part way through the meal, had finished the main course and were tucking into the sweet course, looking forward to mince pies, chocolates and coffee, when the front doorbell rang. I went to answer the door and before I even got there, I had a surprise. Since our front door is glazed, I could see through the glass and there stood Santa Claus, complete with the whole Santa regalia, including a large full sack. I opened the door. I wasn't expecting Santa Claus to arrive that night and was even less expecting his first words to me which were, "Hello, am I in the right place?"

I didn't know whether he was in the right place; I didn't know what place he was looking for, so I said, "Well, what are you looking for?" and he replied, "I've got a sack full of presents for a lot of ladies," and I said, "Well, we've got a lot of ladies here at the moment, about thirty or forty ladies."

"Right," he answered, "it must be the right place."

So, without more ado, he comes in, he goes into the dining room, where everyone is eating or drinking and, there is a lot of "Ho Ho-ing!" and "Hum Humming!" and a lot of hugs and 'Merry Christmases' and much laughter and everybody gets a present, including me. I still have my present; it's a nice little satin covered notebook which occasionally makes an appearance - several times it's been used on stage as a 'prop' in shows. At the end of Santa's visit there was more hugging and waving of goodbye, and more "Thank you-ing" and "Merry Christmas-ing" and all was very jolly. Nobody made any comment about the fact that Santa had called, except to say what fun his visit had been, so, I assumed that he had been in the right place, and all was well. It was not until the next day that it occurred to me, since there had been two group secretaries, even if neither of them had organised the Santa Claus, each would reasonably assume that the other one had, or they would both assume that I had, and I most definitely hadn't. I'm sorry to say, or delighted to say that, to this day, I have no idea at all whether Santa Claus *was* in the right place.

Thank you for listening and I hope you have a Merry Christmas. Bye-bye.